RICHMOND
Picture Dictionary
ENGLISH

Santillana USA
www.santillanausa.com

D1473409

© 2004, Santillana USA Publishing Company, Inc.
2023 NW 84th Avenue, Miami, FL 33122

Published by Richmond Publishing® 1997
19 Berghem Mews, Blythe Road, London W14 OHN
© 1995, 1997, Santillana Ediciones Generales, S.L.

Picture Dictionary English
ISBN 10: 1-59437-454-6
ISBN 13: 978-1-59437-454-8

15 14 13 12   8 9 10 11 12 13 14

Printed in the USA by HCI Printing and Publishing, Inc.

CONTENTS

INTRODUCTION 4

VISUAL VOCABULARY

DICTIONARY 89

INTRODUCTION

The **Richmond Picture Dictionary** has been designed for young learners to use independently at home or in the classroom during their first years of studying English. The dictionary is intended to help learners establish an immediate association between vocabulary and a visual image, thereby reducing dependence upon translation. It offers students the opportunity to increase and enrich their English vocabulary first through association with the illustrations in the picture section, then with clear English-only explanations in the alphabetical dictionary section.

VISUAL VOCABULARY

The Visual Vocabulary section presents words within 17 themes which are divided into 72 different sub-categories. The colorful pictures have been generated by computer to provide a three-dimensional appearance and to show each object in great detail. The pictures are clearly labeled with the words for objects, living things, descriptions and actions. Nouns, verbs and adjectives are each illustrated separately.

At home or at school, learners may like to copy elements from particular drawings to make their own vocabulary cards or notes. In the classroom, the teacher can organize games in which first the teacher then the students describe an object and its location in the picture, and ask other students to name it.

DAN AND PAM

Dan and Pam are the two characters that appear on almost every page of the Visual Vocabulary section. Their purpose is to represent actions relevant to the topic on each page, and to reinforce meaning through gestures and expressions.

The teacher can take advantage of the actions shown by Dan and Pam for role-playing, TPR or other dramatization activities, or for the development of narratives.

DICTIONARY

In the Dictionary section, all the words that appear in the Visual Vocabulary are listed alphabetically, with a clear explanation of each word in English. The explanations use simple language based around synonyms, antonyms, description, contextualization and usage. Grammatical terms are not used.

Each word is defined as it is shown in the pictures, and secondary meanings are not introduced. Page references are given for all definitions so that these can immediately be referred to in case of doubt.

Teachers can use the definition given for each word for word games and quizzes.

As a follow-up activity, the teacher can read out the definitions for a particular lexical group, and invite students in pairs or teams to guess the corresponding words. Learners can also use the definitions, or invent their own following the models given, for making up their own crossword puzzles, wordsearches, etc.

VISUAL
VOCABULARY

THE BODY
Parts of the Body

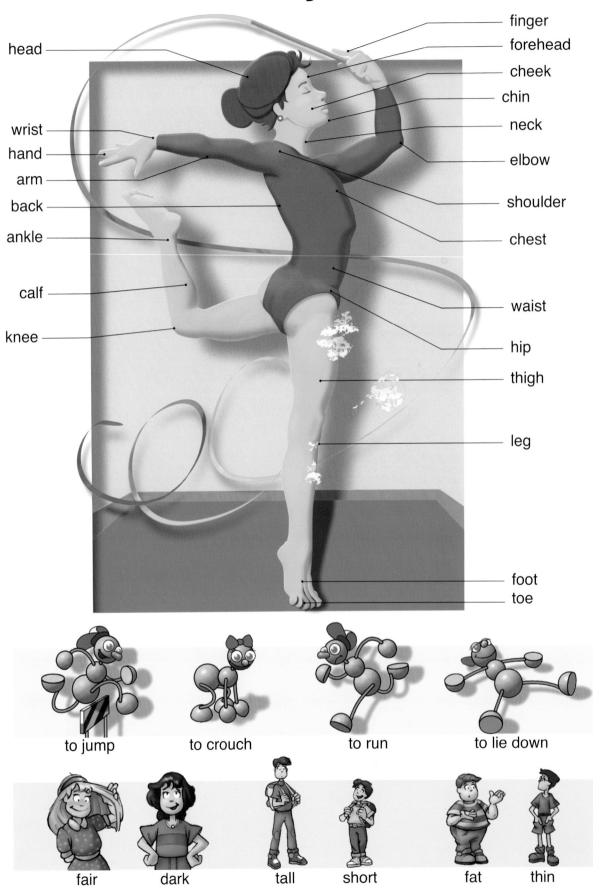

head

finger
forehead
cheek
chin
neck
elbow

wrist
hand
arm
back
ankle

shoulder

chest

calf

waist

knee

hip

thigh

leg

foot
toe

to jump   to crouch   to run   to lie down

fair   dark   tall   short   fat   thin

The Skeleton and the Muscles

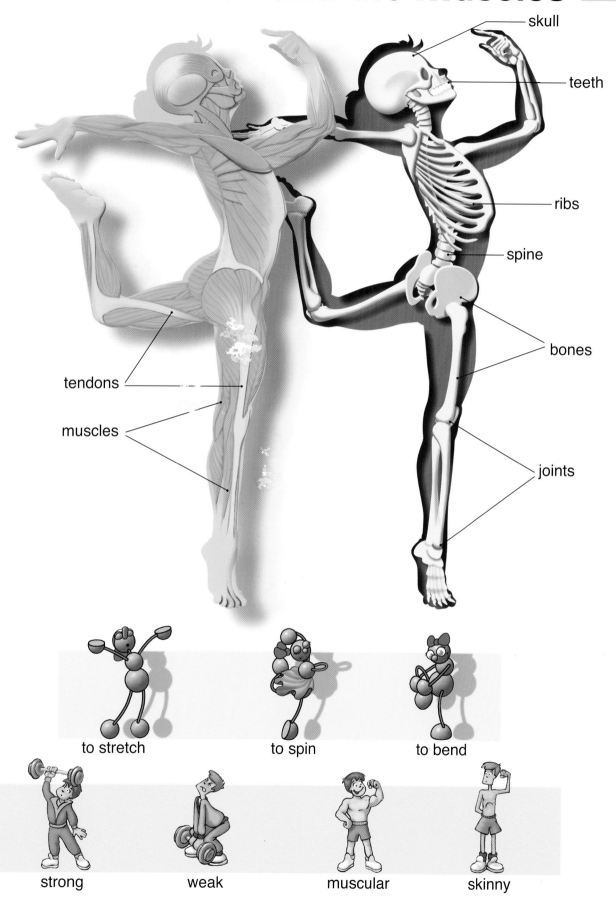

skull

teeth

ribs

spine

bones

joints

tendons

muscles

to stretch

to spin

to bend

strong

weak

muscular

skinny

The Senses

sense of hearing

ear

sense of smell

nose

nostril

sense of touch

skin

to touch

to taste

to see

to hear

to smell

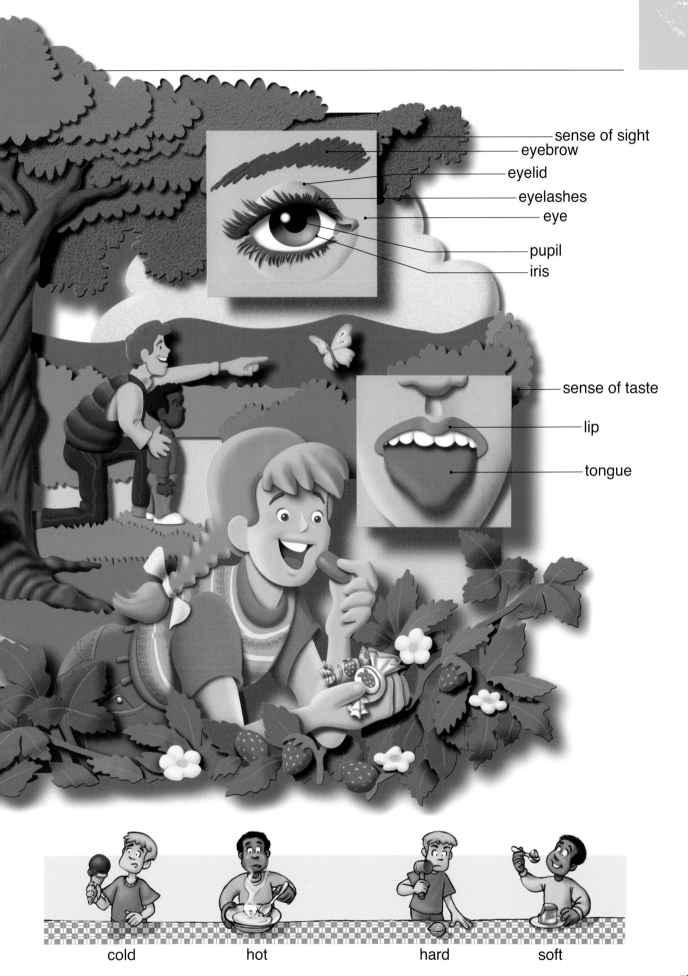

sense of sight

eyebrow

eyelid

eyelashes

eye

pupil

iris

sense of taste

lip

tongue

cold

hot

hard

soft

A Family

father

mother

uncle

aunt

grandfather

son

grandmother

cousin

sister

brother

to love   to shout   to laugh   to cry

young   old   happy   sad   quiet   noisy

waaah!

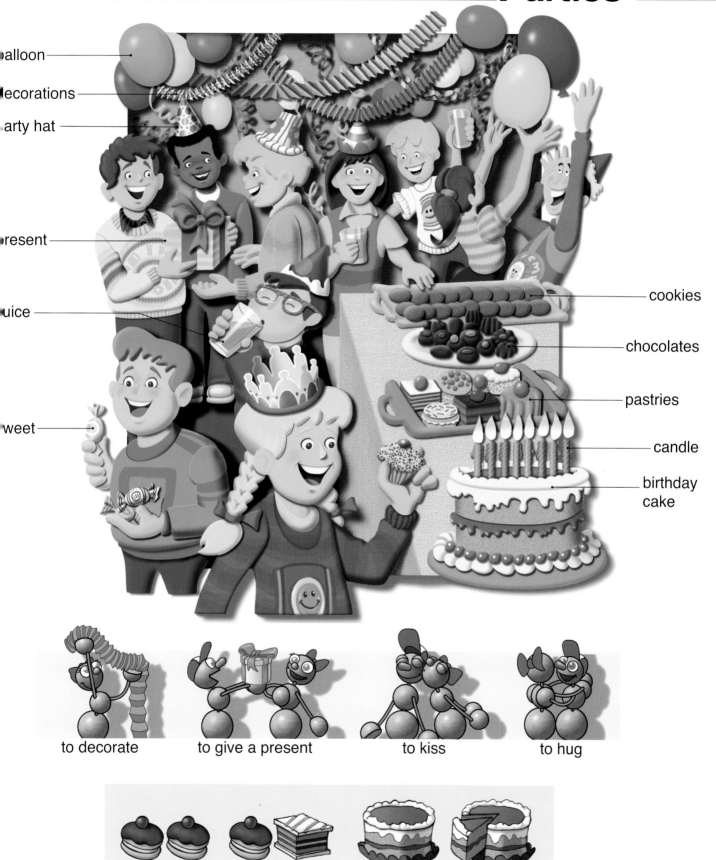

balloon

decorations

party hat

present

juice

sweet

cookies

chocolates

pastries

candle

birthday cake

to decorate

to give a present

to kiss

to hug

the same

different

whole

slice

CLOTHES
Daytime

hat

cardigan

shirt

belt

skirt

tights

shoe

cap

jacket

sweater

pants

sock

sneaker

to get dressed

to get undressed

to button

to unbutton

short

long

wrinkled

ironed

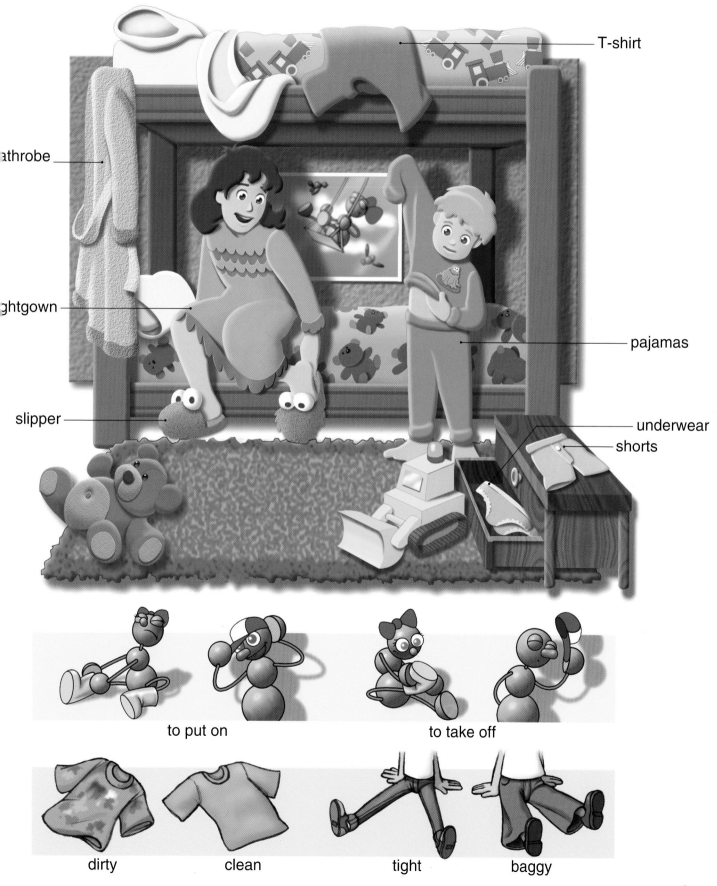

T-shirt

athrobe

ghtgown

pajamas

slipper

underwear

shorts

to put on

to take off

dirty

clean

tight

baggy

THE HOUSE
Outside

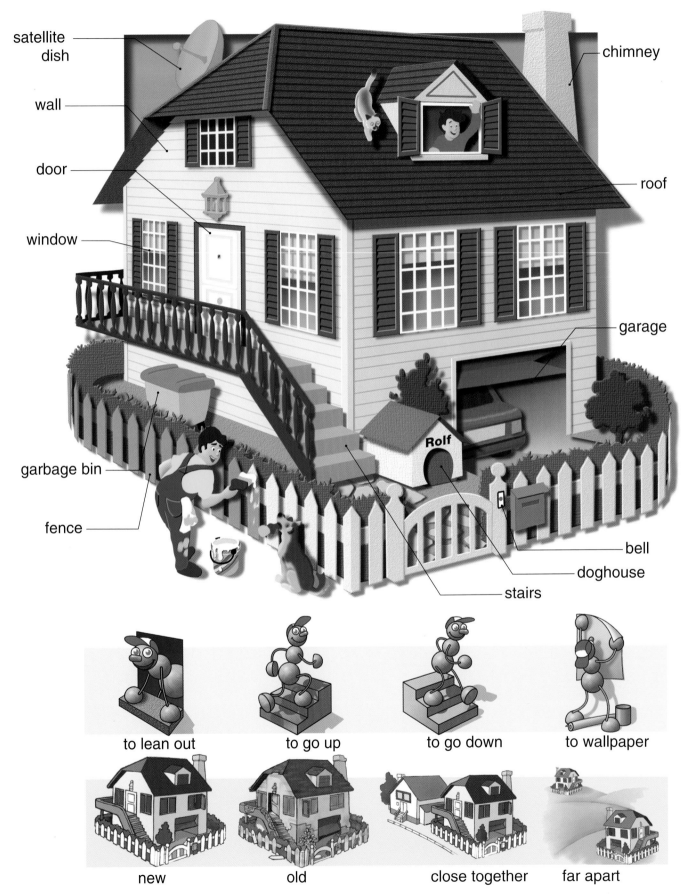

satellite dish

wall

door

window

garbage bin

fence

chimney

roof

garage

bell

doghouse

stairs

Rolf

to lean out

to go up

to go down

to wallpaper

new

old

close together

far apart

The Living Room

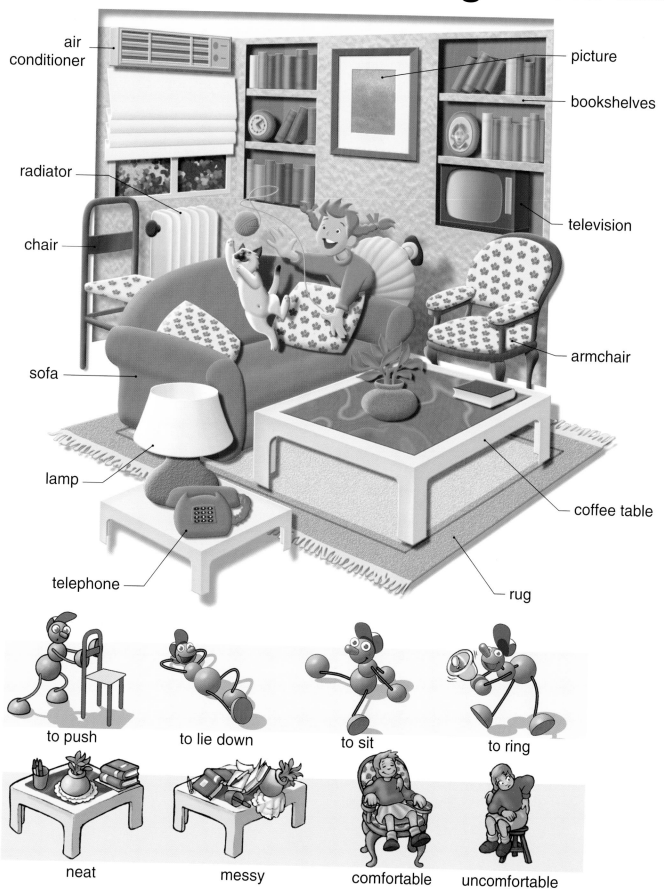

air conditioner

picture

bookshelves

radiator

television

chair

armchair

sofa

lamp

coffee table

telephone

rug

to push

to lie down

to sit

to ring

neat

messy

comfortable

uncomfortable

The Bedroom

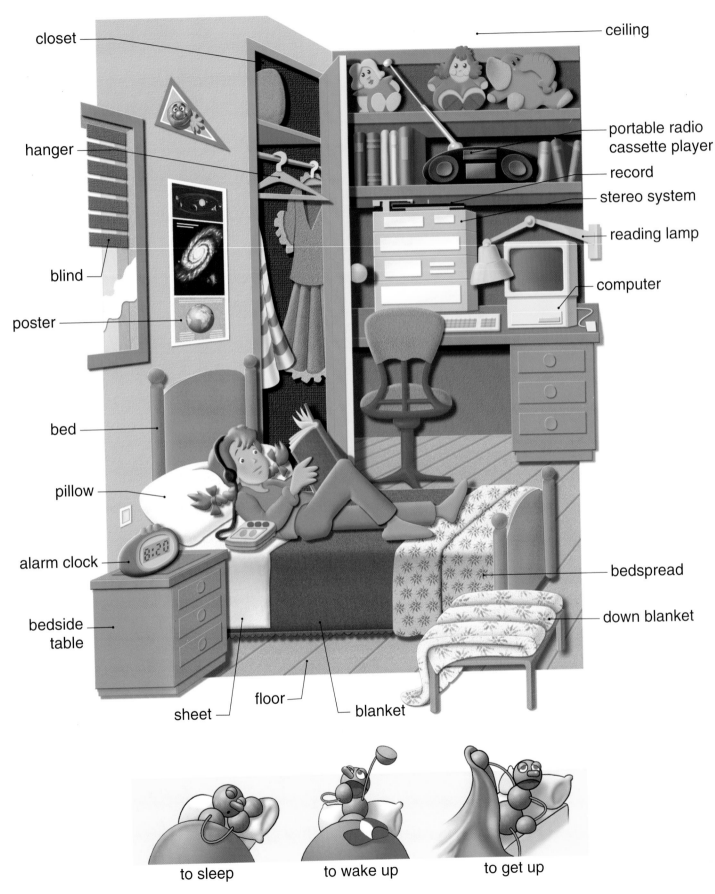

closet

ceiling

hanger

portable radio cassette player

blind

record

stereo system

poster

reading lamp

computer

bed

pillow

alarm clock

bedspread

bedside table

down blanket

sheet

floor

blanket

to sleep

to wake up

to get up

The Bathroom

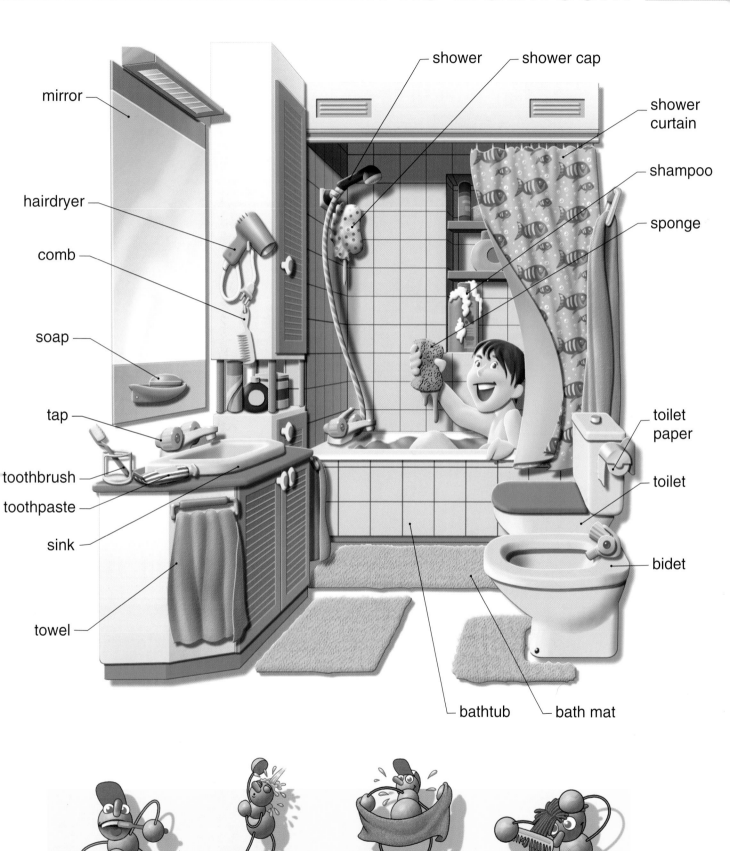

mirror

hairdryer

comb

soap

tap

toothbrush

toothpaste

sink

towel

shower — shower cap

shower curtain

shampoo

sponge

toilet paper

toilet

bidet

bathtub — bath mat

to brush your teeth   to take a shower   to dry yourself   to comb your hair

The Kitchen

vase

mixer

coffee-maker

blender

washing machine

grater

table

corkscrew

can-opener

sink

refrigerator

fork

glass

soup dish

plate

bowl

knife

spoon

to stir

to grate

to cut

to chop

microwave oven

toaster

dishwasher

cupboard

utensils

tray

stove

ladle

serving dish

pitcher

teapot

sugar bowl

teaspoon

tureen

bread basket

cup

table cloth

napkin

to wash

to peel

to whisk

to fry

19

WORDS TO DESCRIBE POSITION
Where Are They?

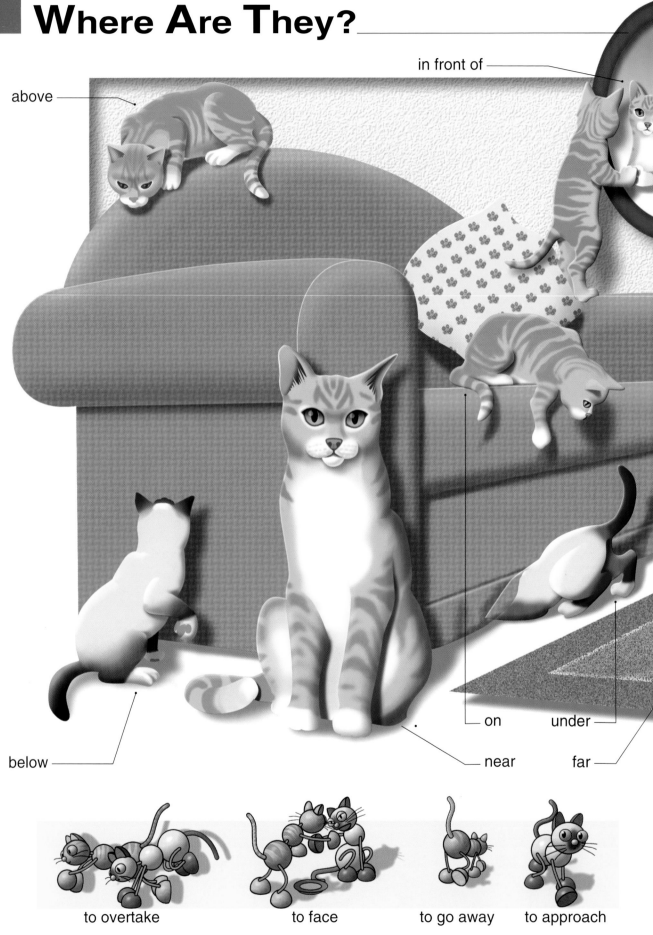

above

in front of

below

on

near

under

far

to overtake

to face

to go away

to approach

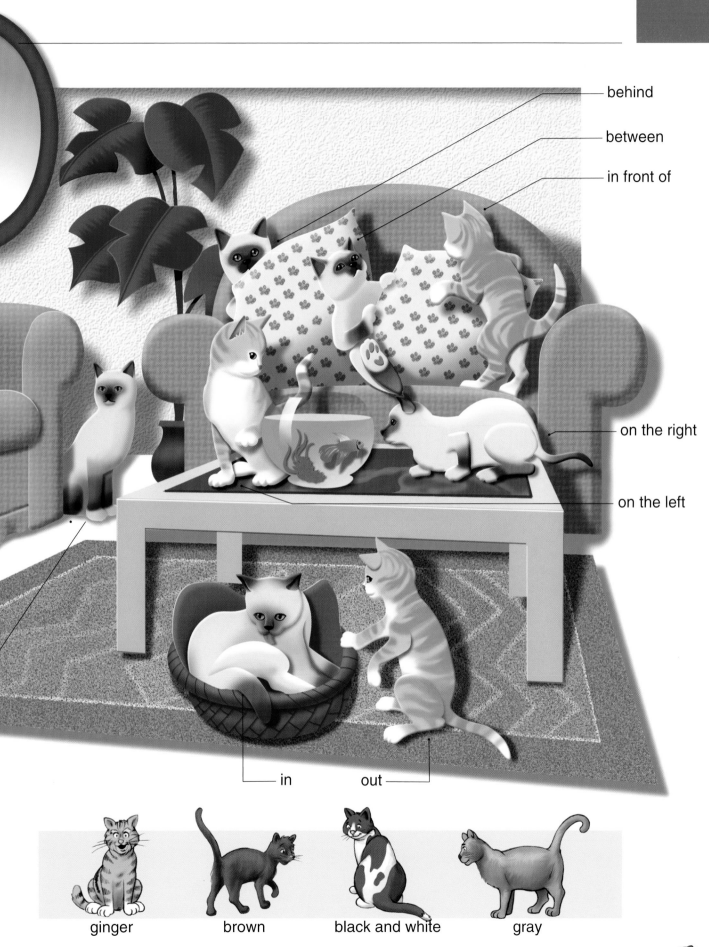

behind

between

in front of

on the right

on the left

in

out

ginger

brown

black and white

gray

SCHOOL
The Classroom

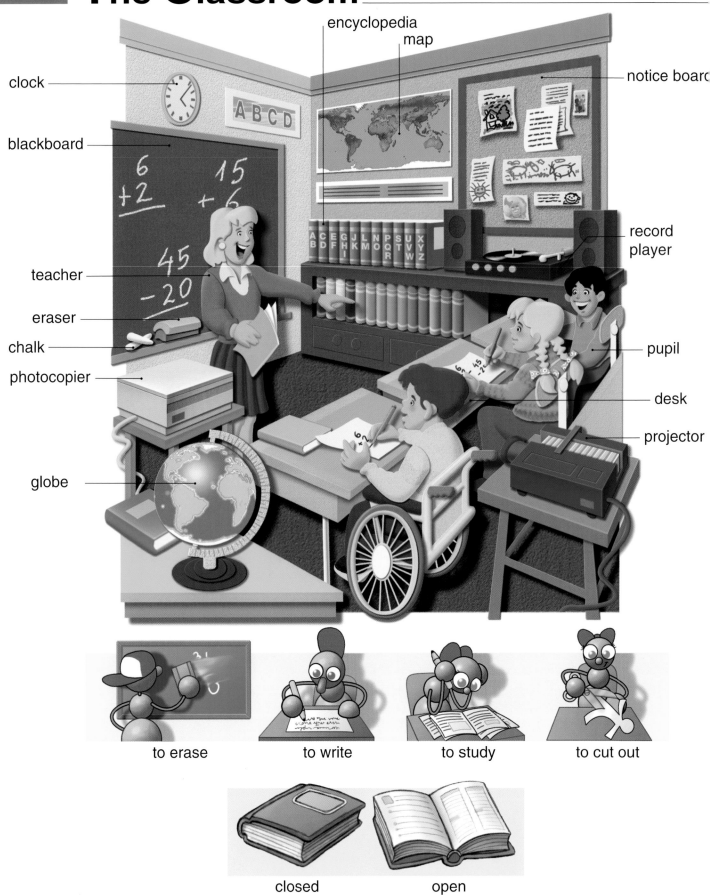

encyclopedia

map

clock

notice board

blackboard

A B C D

record player

teacher

eraser

chalk

pupil

photocopier

desk

projector

globe

to erase

to write

to study

to cut out

closed

open

School Objects

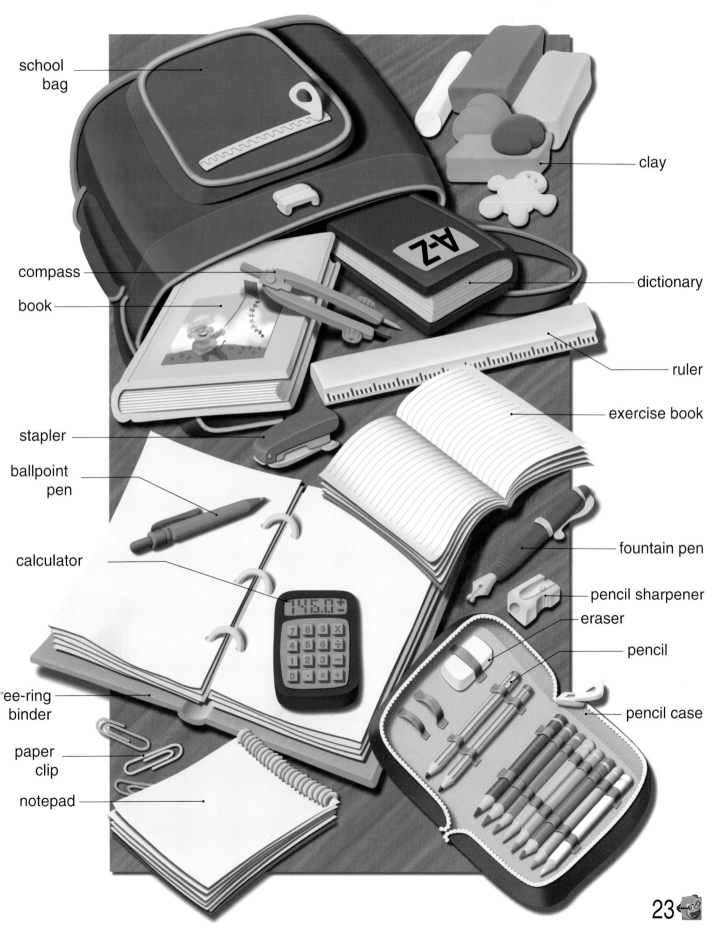

school bag

clay

compass

dictionary

book

ruler

exercise book

stapler

ballpoint pen

calculator

fountain pen

pencil sharpener

eraser

pencil

ee-ring binder

pencil case

paper clip

notepad

Colors

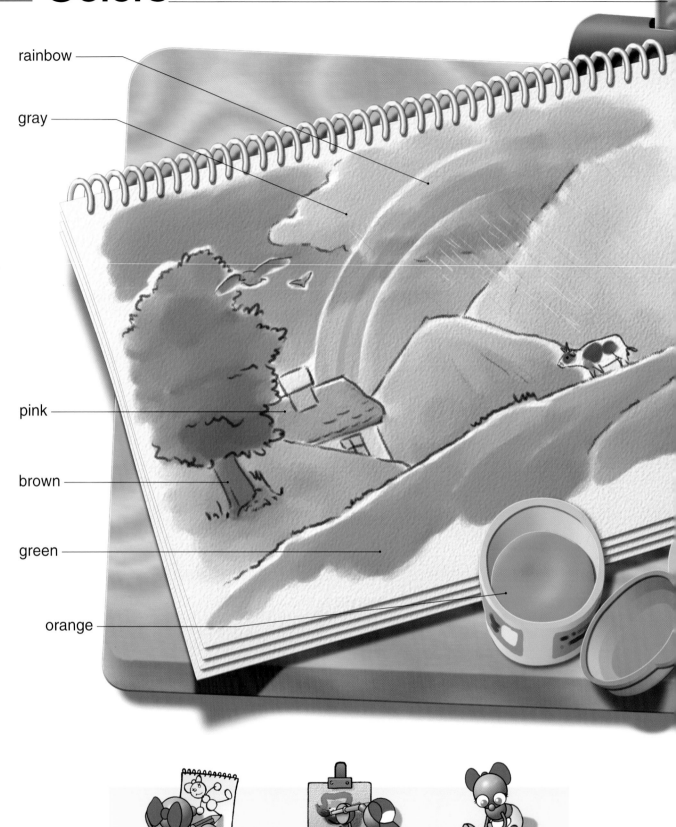

rainbow

gray

pink

brown

green

orange

to draw

to paint

to scribble

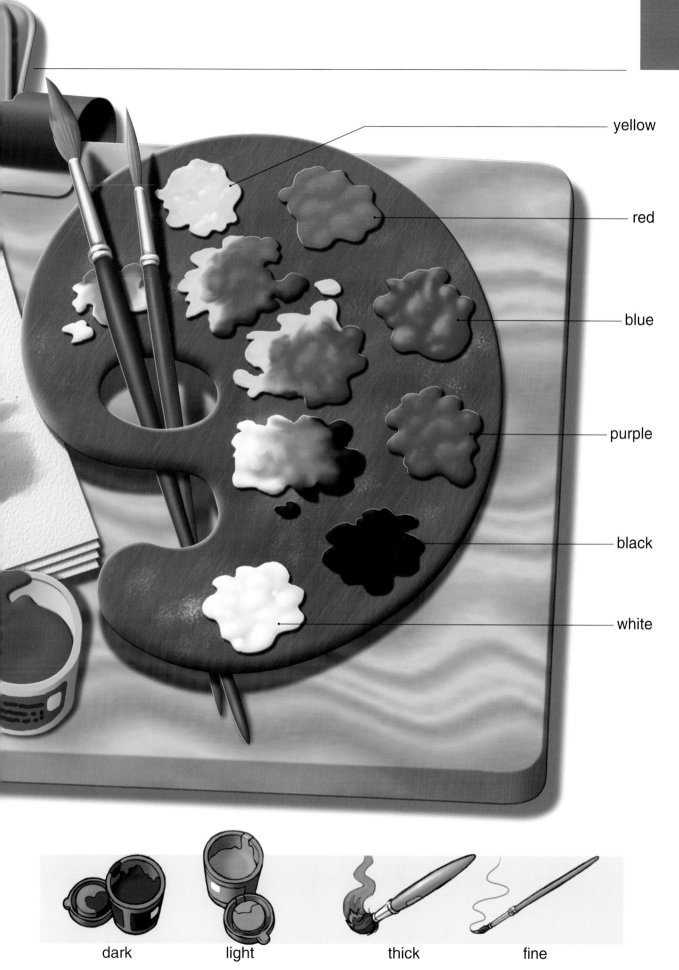

yellow

red

blue

purple

black

white

dark

light

thick

fine

25

Numbers and Shapes

first   second   third   fourth   fifth

1 2 3 4 5 6 7 8 9 10

one   two   three   four   five   six   seven   eight   nine   ten

11 12 13 14 15 16 17 18 19 20

eleven   twelve   thirteen   fourteen   fifteen   sixteen   seventeen   eighteen   nineteen   twenty

30 40 50 60 70 80 90 100

thirty   forty   fifty   sixty   seventy   eighty   ninety   one hundred

1.000   1.000.000

one thousand   one million

to add   to subtract   to multiply   to divide

sixth seventh eighth ninth tenth

square

rectangle

circle

triangle

cube

sphere

cone

round rectangular triangular square

Dinosaurs

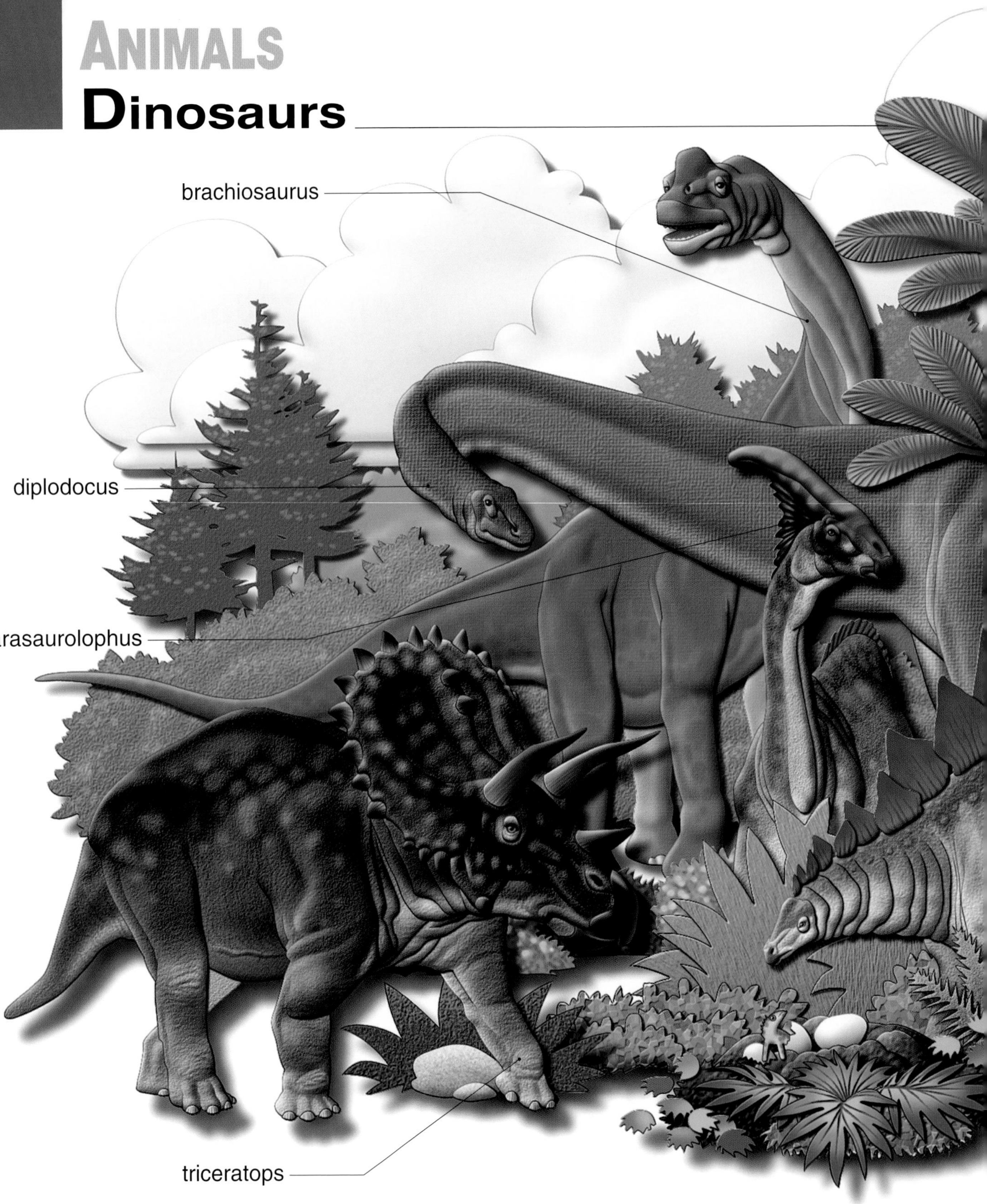

brachiosaurus

diplodocus

parasaurolophus

triceratops

to hatch

to swim

to fly

to die

archaeopteryx

tyrannosaurus

stegosaurus

compsognathus

carnivorous   herbivorous   light   heavy   gigantic

The Cat and the Dog

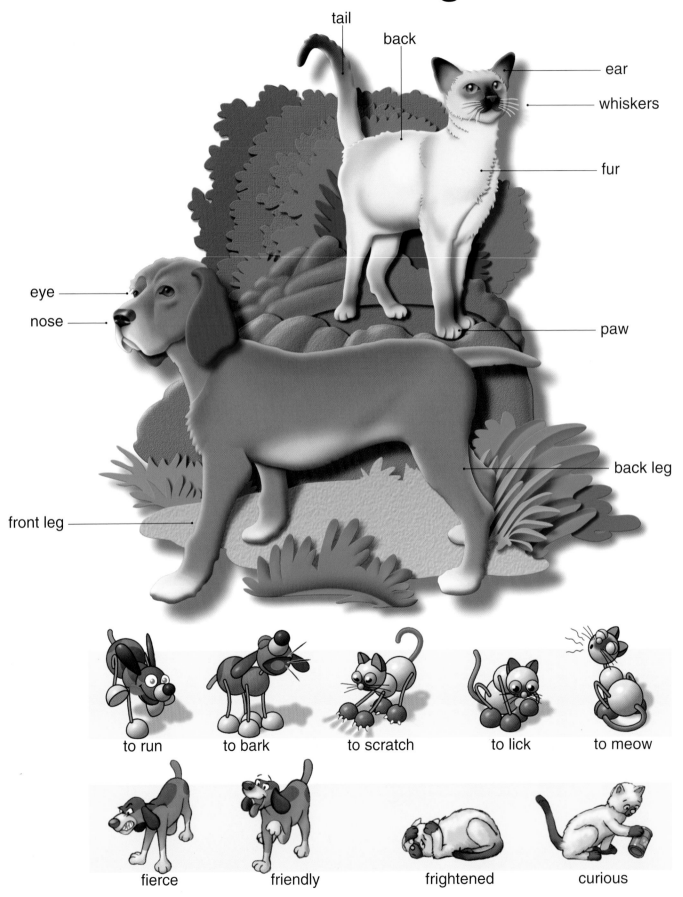

tail

back

ear

whiskers

fur

eye

nose

paw

back leg

front leg

to run

to bark

to scratch

to lick

to meow

fierce

friendly

frightened

curious

The Horse and the Camel

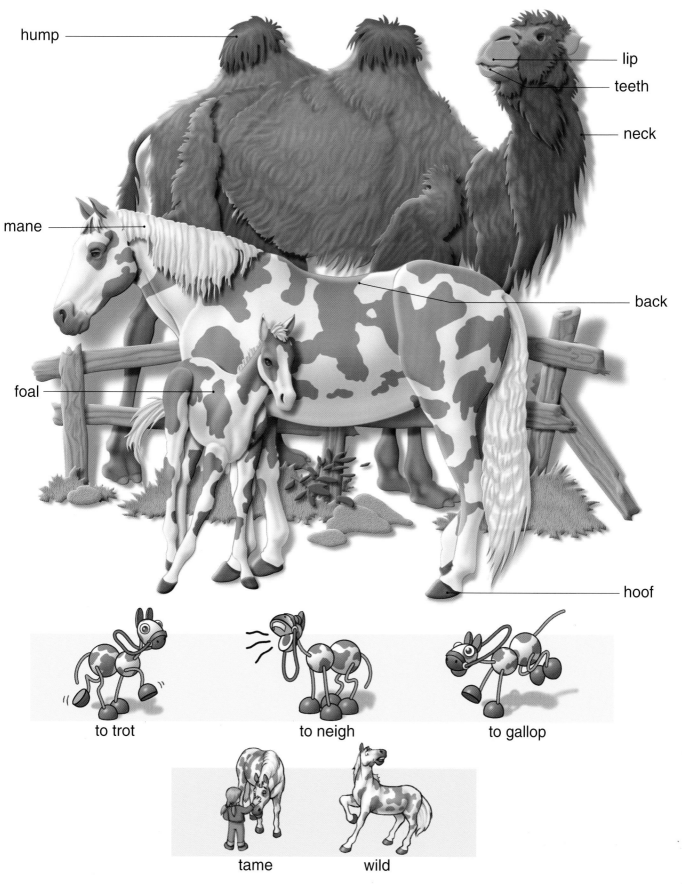

hump

lip

teeth

neck

mane

back

foal

hoof

to trot

to neigh

to gallop

tame

wild

The Sheep and the Cow

pen

wool

flock

lamb

horn

hide

udder

hoof

calf

to moo

to milk

to bleat

to shear

woolly

playful

obedient

The Hen and the Sparrow

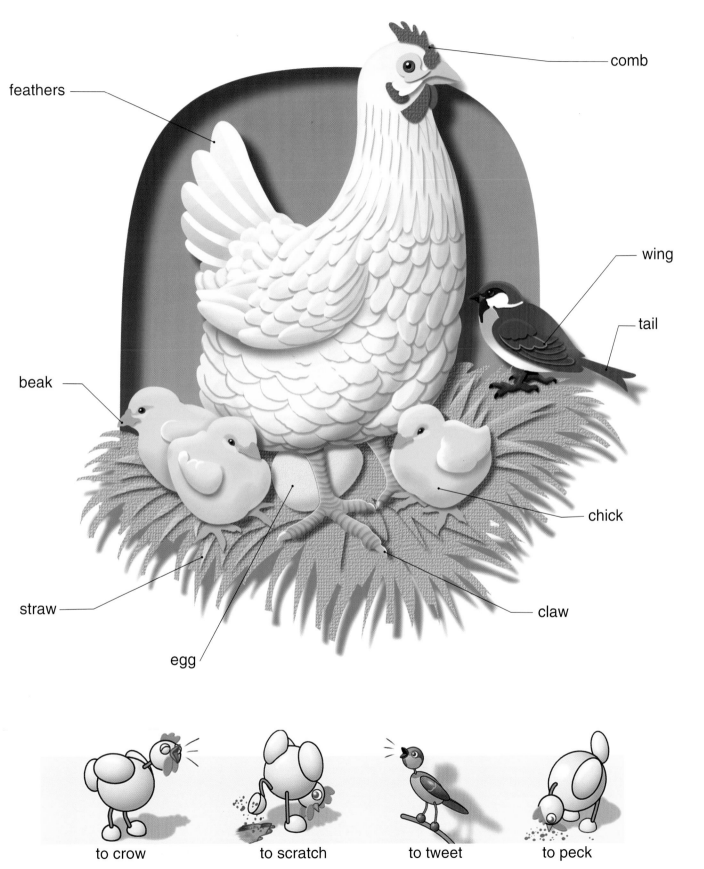

comb

feathers

wing

tail

beak

chick

straw

claw

egg

to crow

to scratch

to tweet

to peck

33

The Snake and the Tortoise

tongue

scales

tail

shell

eyelid

leg

claw

to slither   to coil   to chase   to escape

slow   poisonous   land animal   marine animal

The Shark and the Sardine

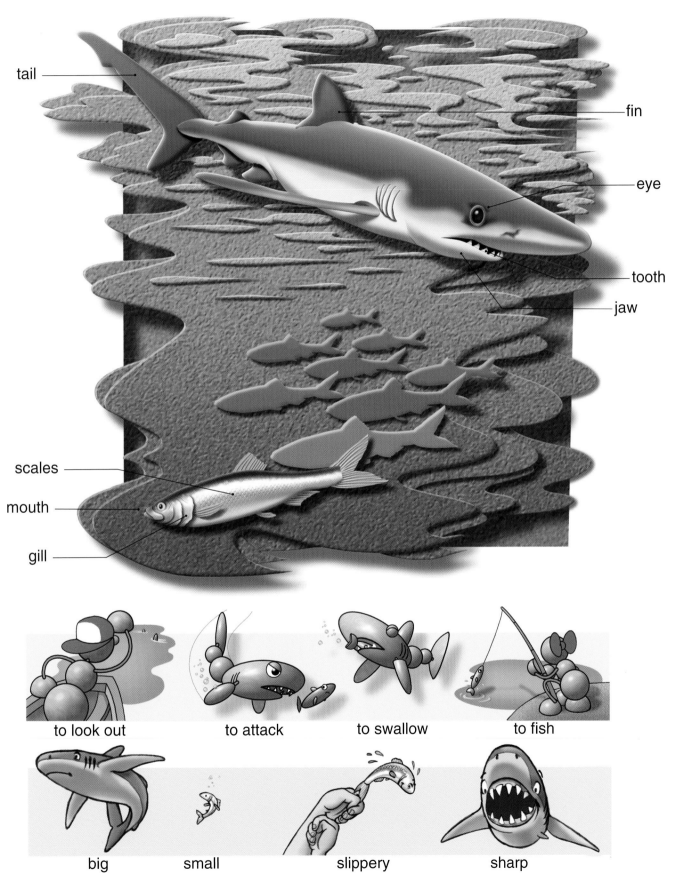

tail

fin

eye

tooth

jaw

scales

mouth

gill

to look out

to attack

to swallow

to fish

big

small

slippery

sharp

The Frog

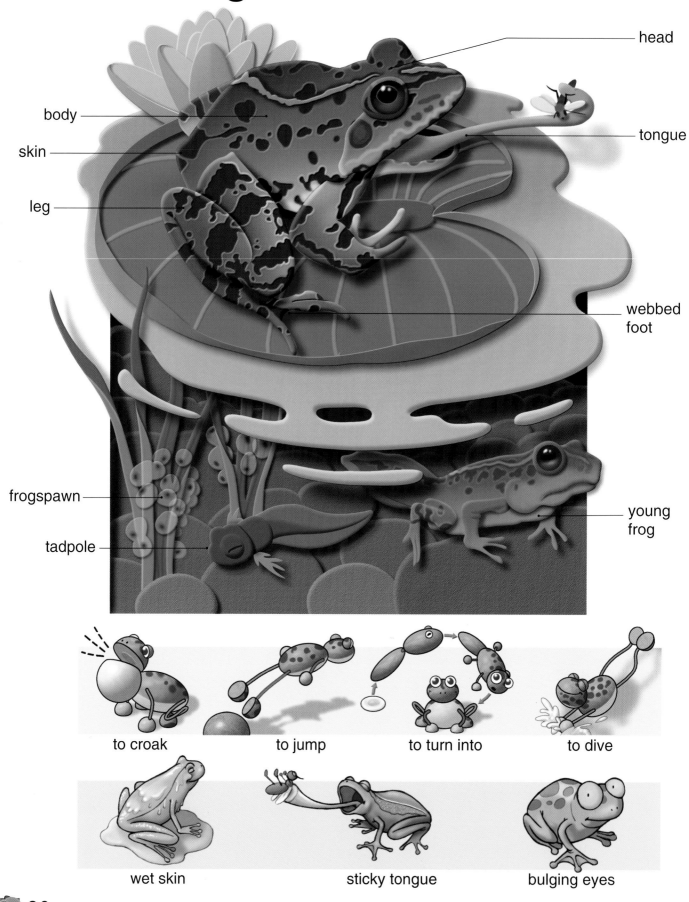

head

body

skin

leg

tongue

webbed foot

frogspawn

tadpole

young frog

to croak

to jump

to turn into

to dive

wet skin

sticky tongue

bulging eyes

36

The Butterfly

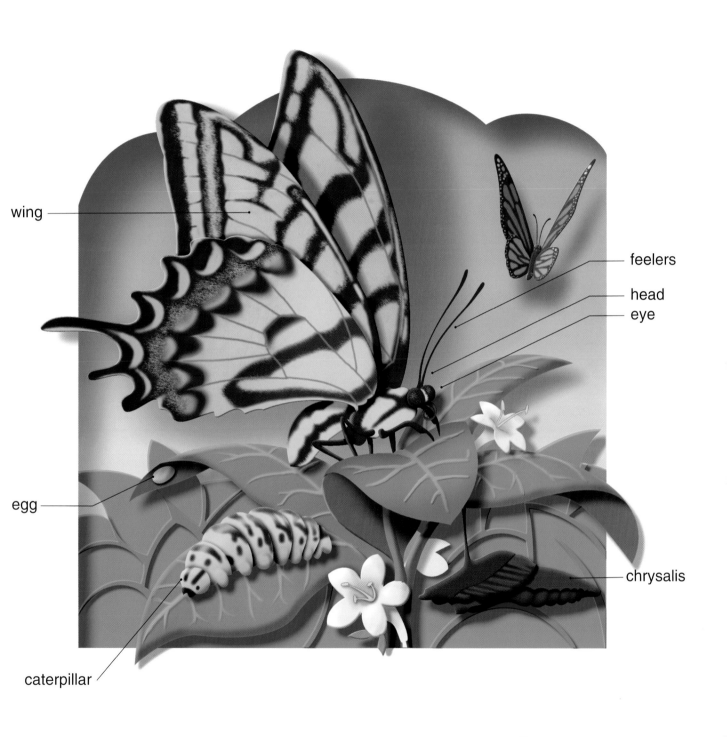

wing

feelers

head

eye

egg

chrysalis

caterpillar

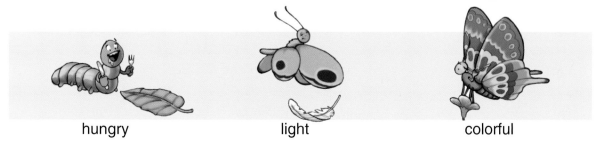

hungry

light

colorful

The Bee

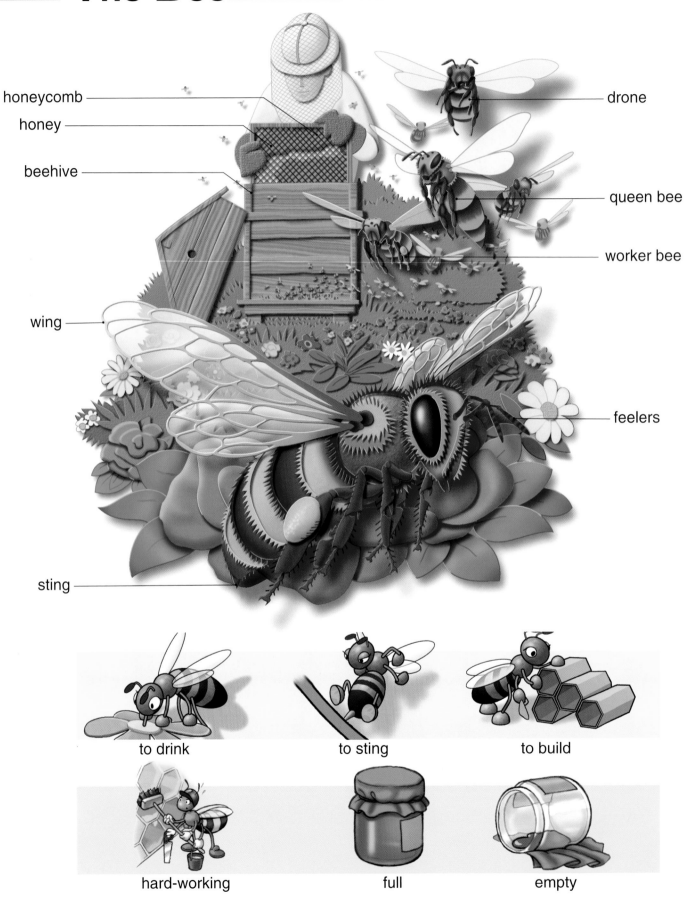

honeycomb

honey

beehive

wing

sting

drone

queen bee

worker bee

feelers

to drink

to sting

to build

hard-working

full

empty

The Octopus and the Snail

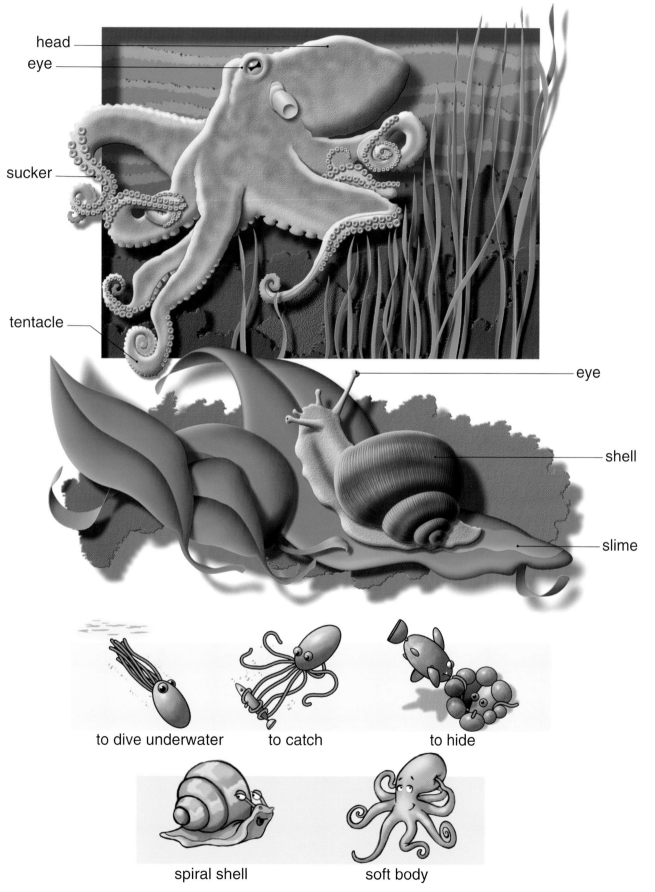

head

eye

sucker

tentacle

eye

shell

slime

to dive underwater   to catch   to hide

spiral shell   soft body

Other Animals

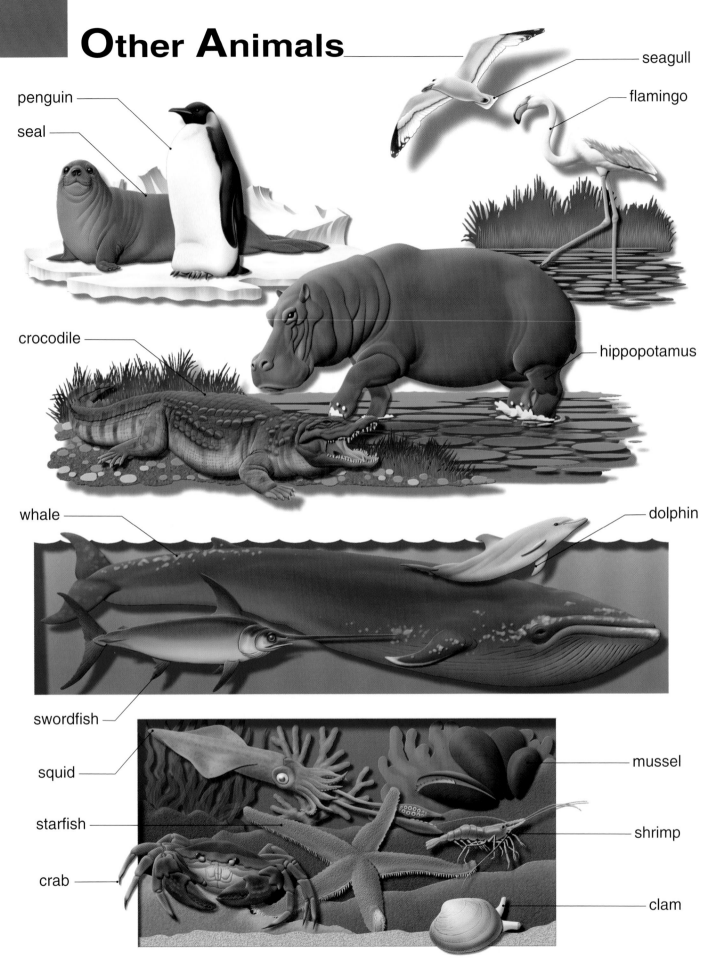

seagull

flamingo

penguin

seal

crocodile

hippopotamus

whale

dolphin

swordfish

squid

mussel

starfish

shrimp

crab

clam

eagle

...and More Animals

giraffe

gorilla

parrot

bear

kangaroo

zebra   elephant   wolf   ostrich   wild boar

hyena   leopard   lion   tiger

Trees

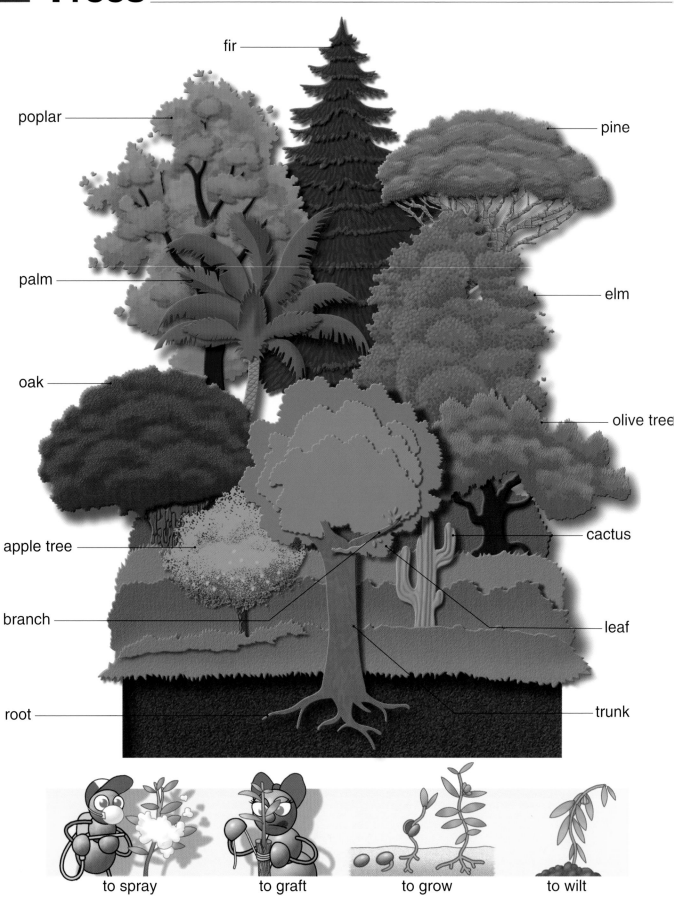

fir

poplar

pine

palm

elm

oak

olive tree

apple tree

cactus

branch

leaf

root

trunk

to spray

to graft

to grow

to wilt

Flowers

petal

carnation

rose

petunia

hydrangea

chrysanthemum

pansy

hyacinth

violet

stalk

daisy

dahlia

tulip

lily

sweet-smelling

pretty

wilted

Fruit and Nuts

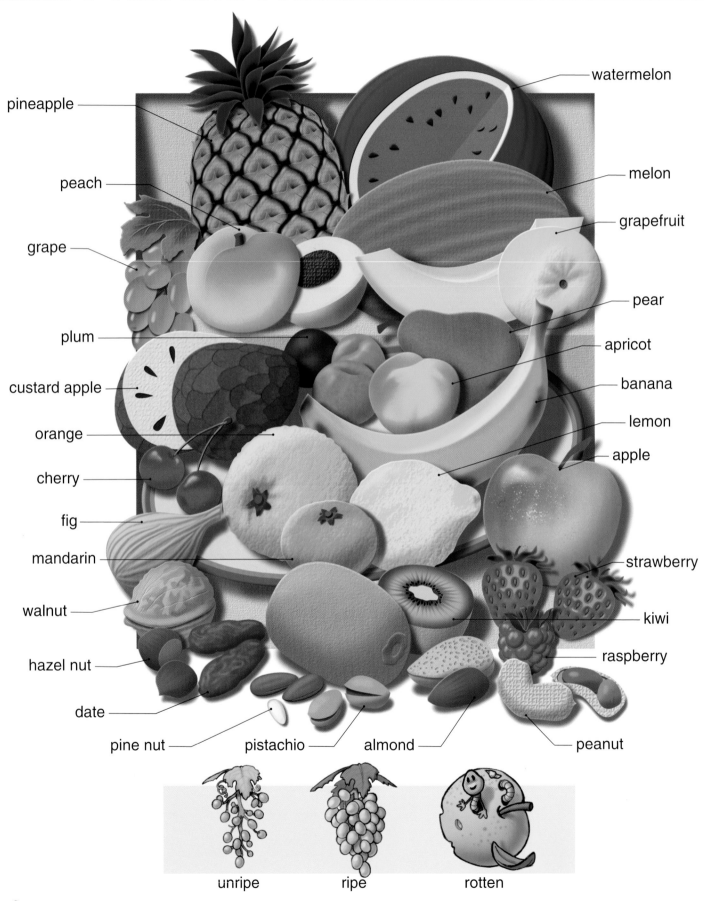

watermelon

pineapple

melon

peach

grapefruit

grape

pear

plum

apricot

custard apple

banana

orange

lemon

cherry

apple

fig

mandarin

strawberry

walnut

kiwi

hazel nut

raspberry

date

pine nut   pistachio   almond   peanut

unripe   ripe   rotten

Vegetables, Legumes and Cereals

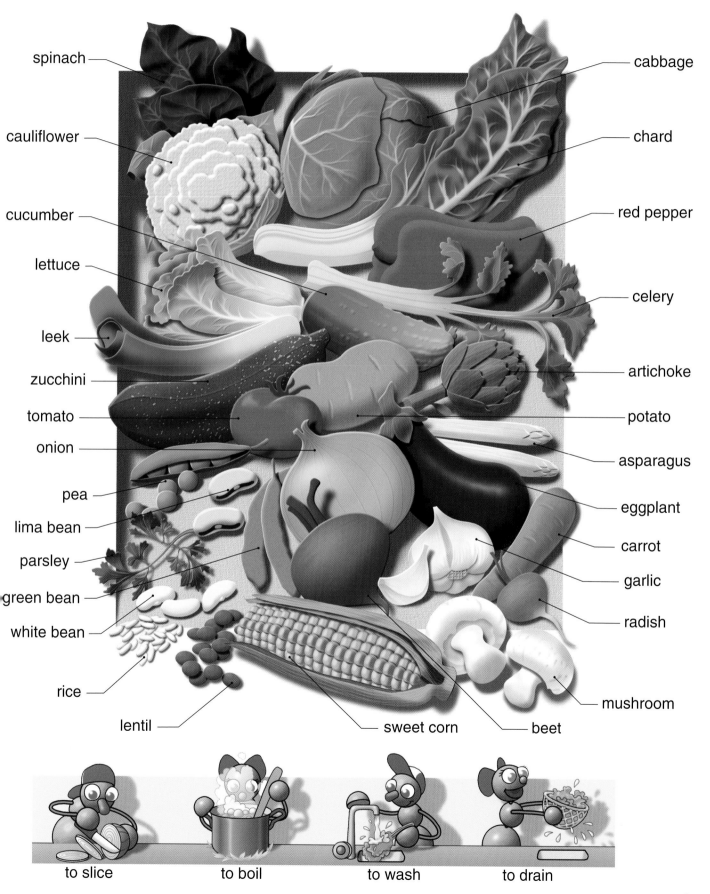

spinach

cabbage

cauliflower

chard

cucumber

red pepper

lettuce

celery

leek

zucchini

artichoke

tomato

potato

onion

asparagus

pea

eggplant

lima bean

carrot

parsley

garlic

green bean

radish

white bean

rice

mushroom

lentil

sweet corn

beet

to slice

to boil

to wash

to drain

The Garden

greenhouse

shed

fence

flower bed

hedge

flower

grass

seed

earth   gardener   path

tidy

untidy

clipped

Garden Tools

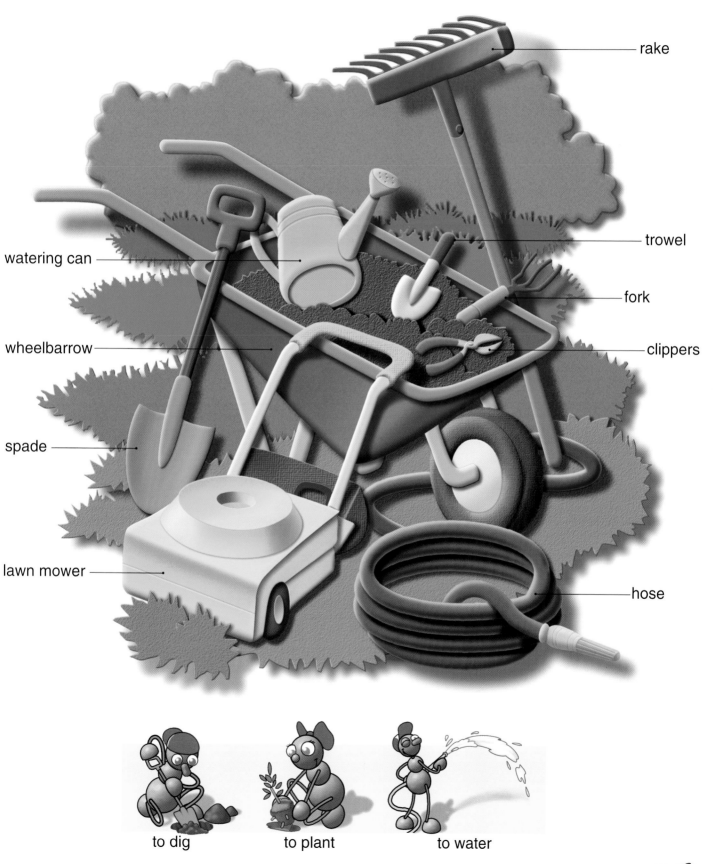

rake

trowel

fork

clippers

watering can

wheelbarrow

spade

lawn mower

hose

to dig

to plant

to water

In the City

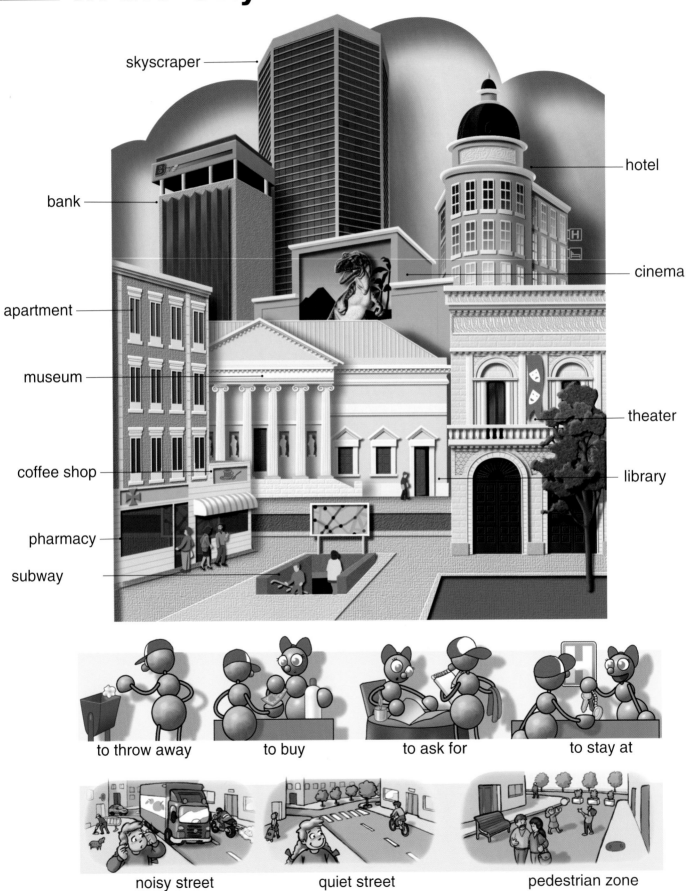

skyscraper

hotel

bank

cinema

apartment

museum

theater

coffee shop

library

pharmacy

subway

to throw away   to buy   to ask for   to stay at

noisy street   quiet street   pedestrian zone

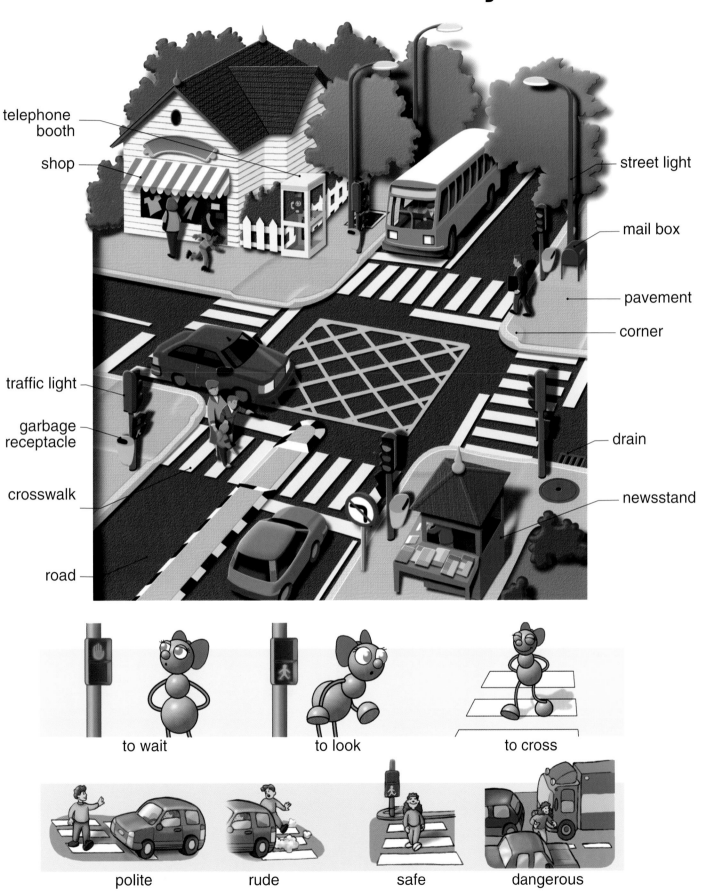

telephone booth

shop

street light

mail box

pavement

corner

traffic light

garbage receptacle

drain

crosswalk

newsstand

road

to wait

to look

to cross

polite

rude

safe

dangerous

On the Road

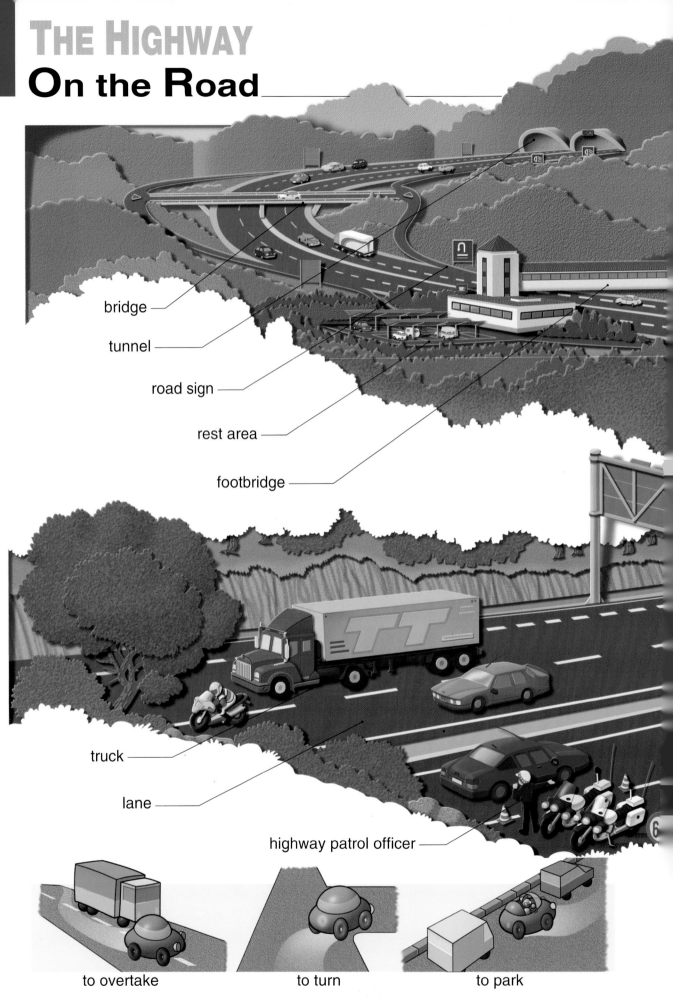

bridge

tunnel

road sign

rest area

footbridge

truck

lane

highway patrol officer

to overtake

to turn

to park

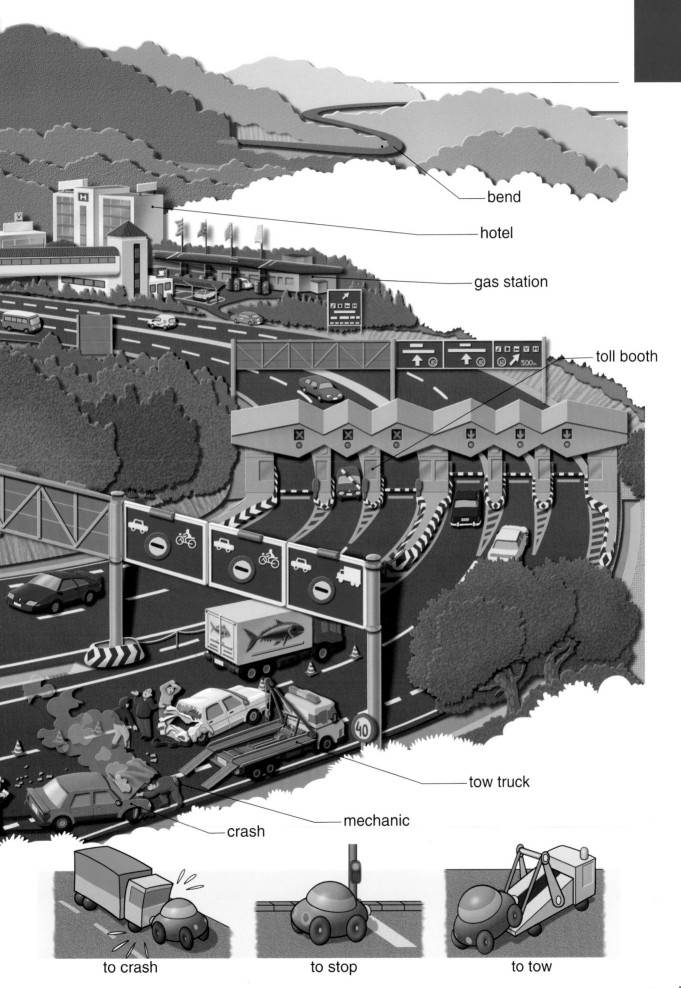

bend

hotel

gas station

toll booth

tow truck

mechanic

crash

to crash

to stop

to tow

Some Jobs

plumber

teacher

veterinarian

bricklayer

lawyer

fish seller

butcher

electrician

greengrocer

to bandage

to work

to rest

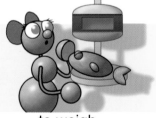
to weigh

pharmacist

fisherman

painter

farmer

reporter

taxi driver

hairdresser

photographer

model

to teach

to fish

to cut

to take photos

The Car

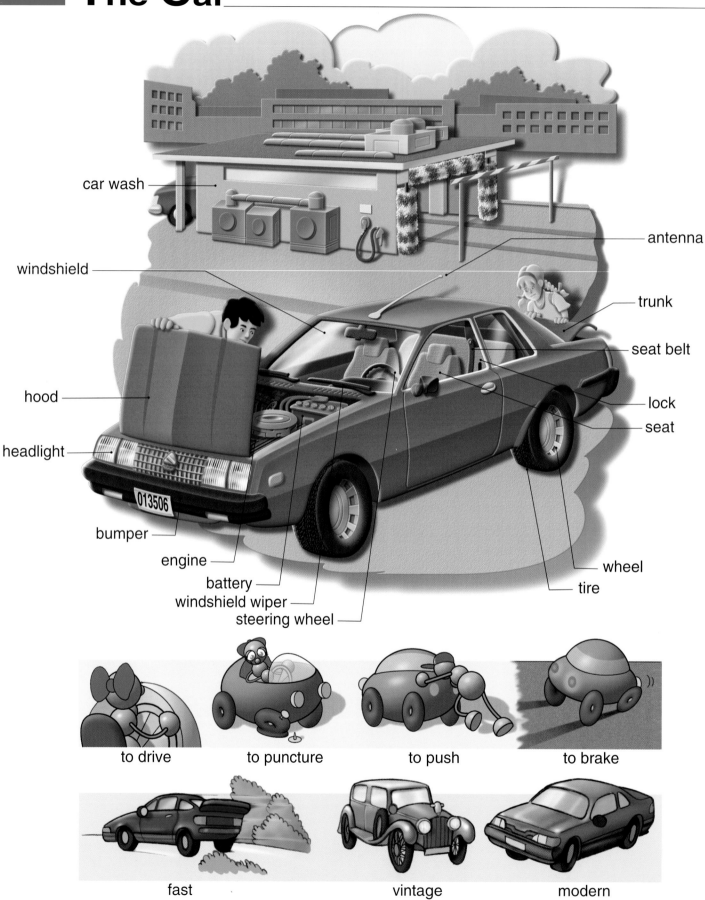

car wash

antenna

windshield

trunk

seat belt

hood

lock

headlight

seat

013506

bumper

engine

wheel

battery

tire

windshield wiper

steering wheel

to drive   to puncture   to push   to brake

fast   vintage   modern

The Bicycle and the Motorcycle

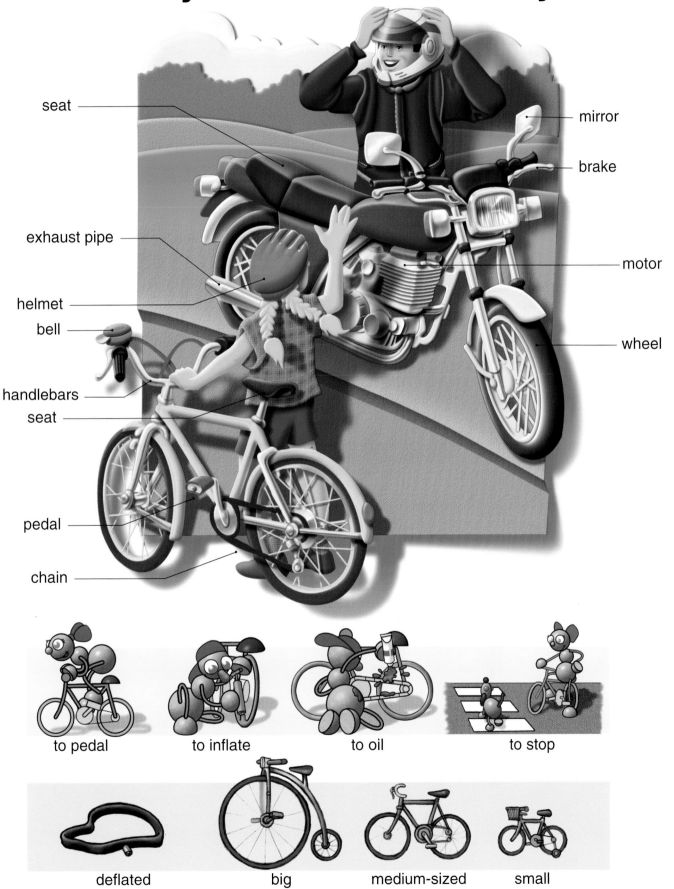

seat

mirror

brake

exhaust pipe

motor

helmet

bell

wheel

handlebars

seat

pedal

chain

to pedal

to inflate

to oil

to stop

deflated

big

medium-sized

small

At the Train Station

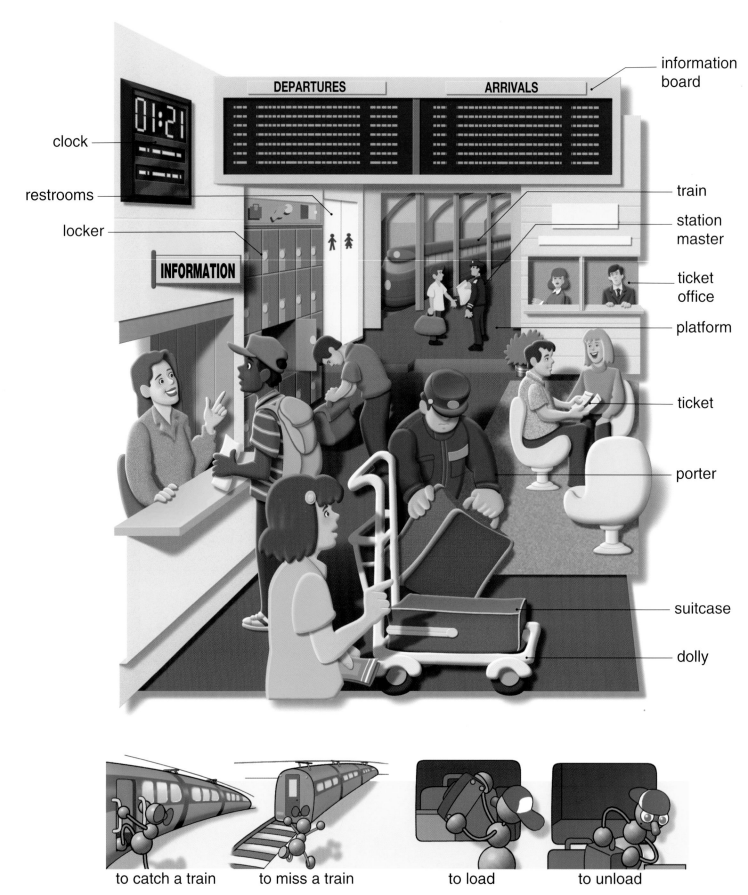

DEPARTURES

ARRIVALS

information board

clock

restrooms

locker

INFORMATION

train

station master

ticket office

platform

ticket

porter

suitcase

dolly

to catch a train   to miss a train   to load   to unload

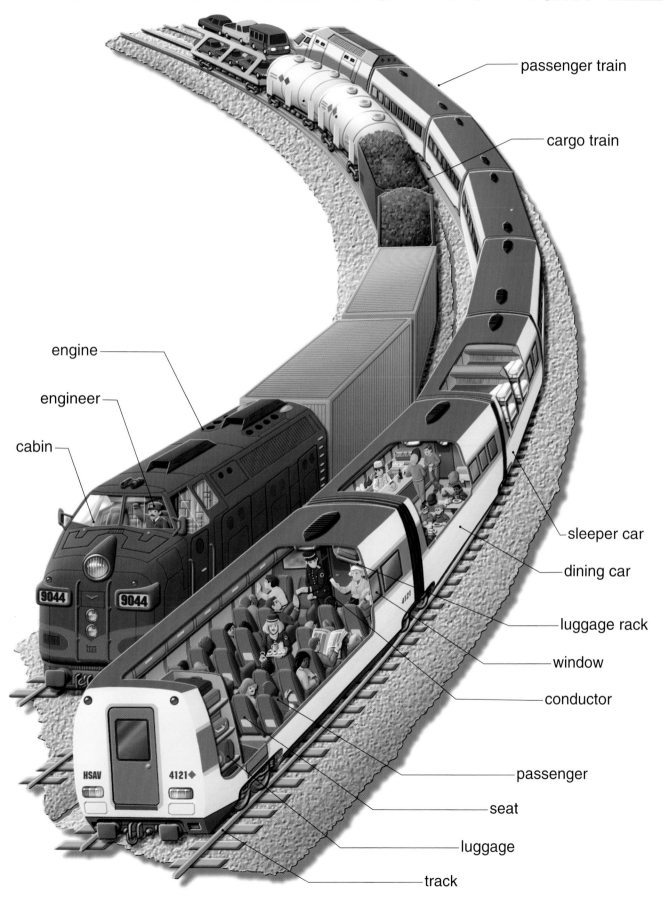

passenger train

cargo train

engine

engineer

cabin

sleeper car

dining car

luggage rack

window

conductor

passenger

seat

luggage

track

At the Airport

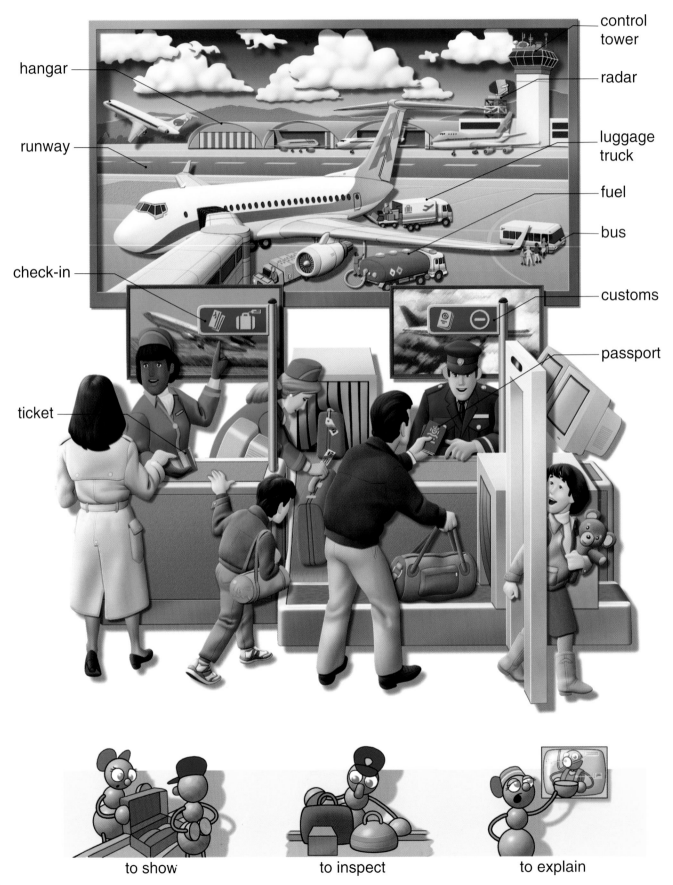

hangar

runway

check-in

ticket

control tower

radar

luggage truck

fuel

bus

customs

passport

to show

to inspect

to explain

On an Airplane

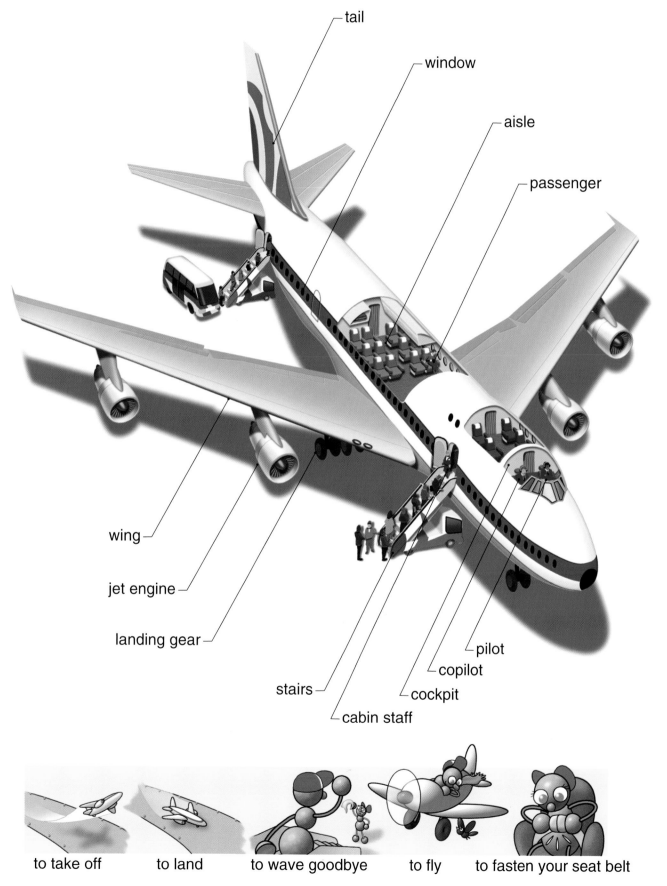

tail

window

aisle

passenger

wing

jet engine

landing gear

pilot

copilot

stairs

cockpit

cabin staff

to take off   to land   to wave goodbye   to fly   to fasten your seat belt

At the Port

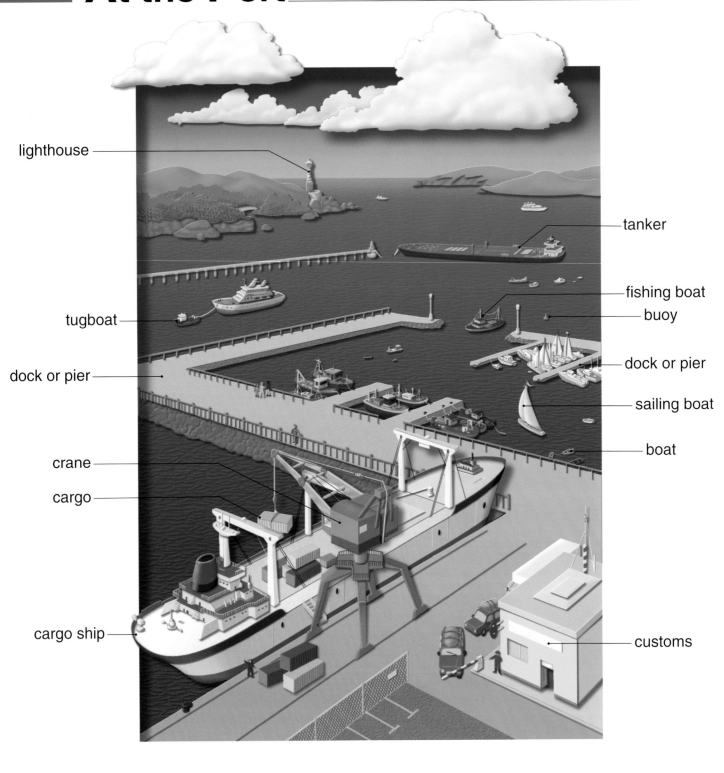

lighthouse

tanker

tugboat

fishing boat

buoy

dock or pier

dock or pier

sailing boat

crane

boat

cargo

cargo ship

customs

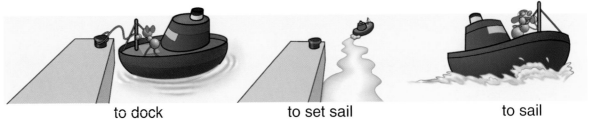

to dock

to set sail

to sail

deck — smokestack — lifeboat — porthole — radar — anchor — prow

stern — rudder — propeller — engine room — hold — cabin

to embark   to disembark   to float   to sink

LEISURE ACTIVITIES
Outdoor Games

kite

swing

seesaw

skateboard

roller skates

hide-and-seek

jump rope

slide

tricycle

marbles

to swing

to skate

to climb

to go down

Indoor Toys and Games

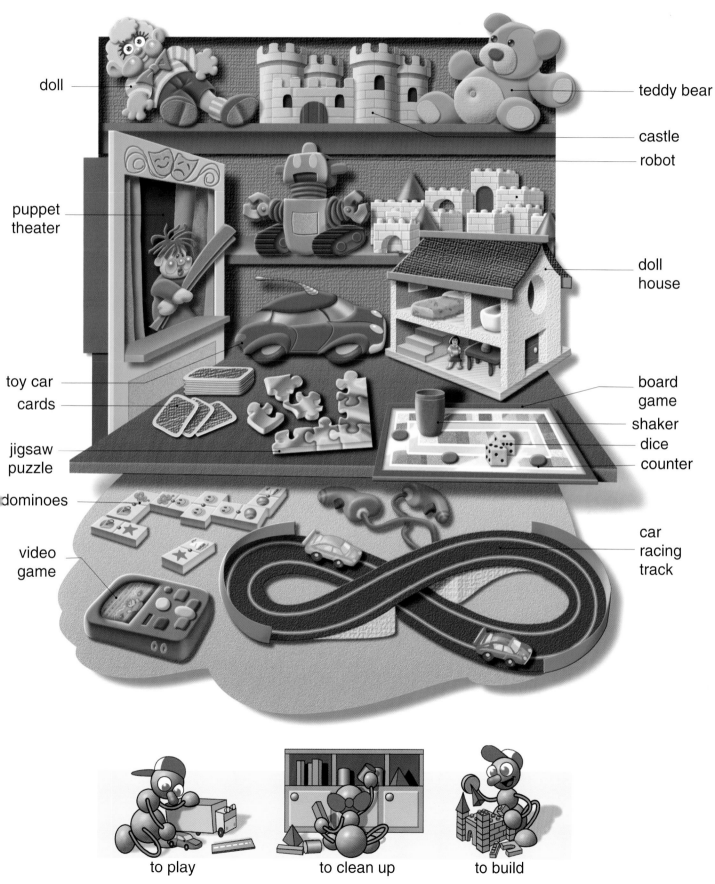

doll

teddy bear

castle

robot

puppet theater

doll house

toy car

cards

board game

shaker

jigsaw puzzle

dice

counter

dominoes

video game

car racing track

to play

to clean up

to build

Electronics and Photography

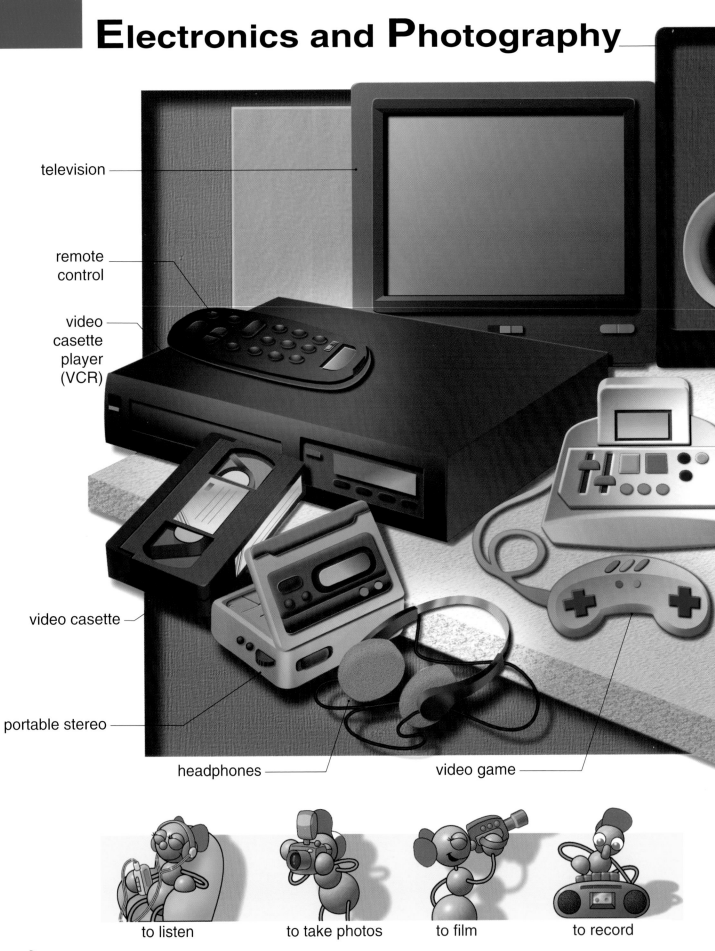

television

remote
control

video
casette
player
(VCR)

video casette

portable stereo

headphones

video game

to listen   to take photos   to film   to record

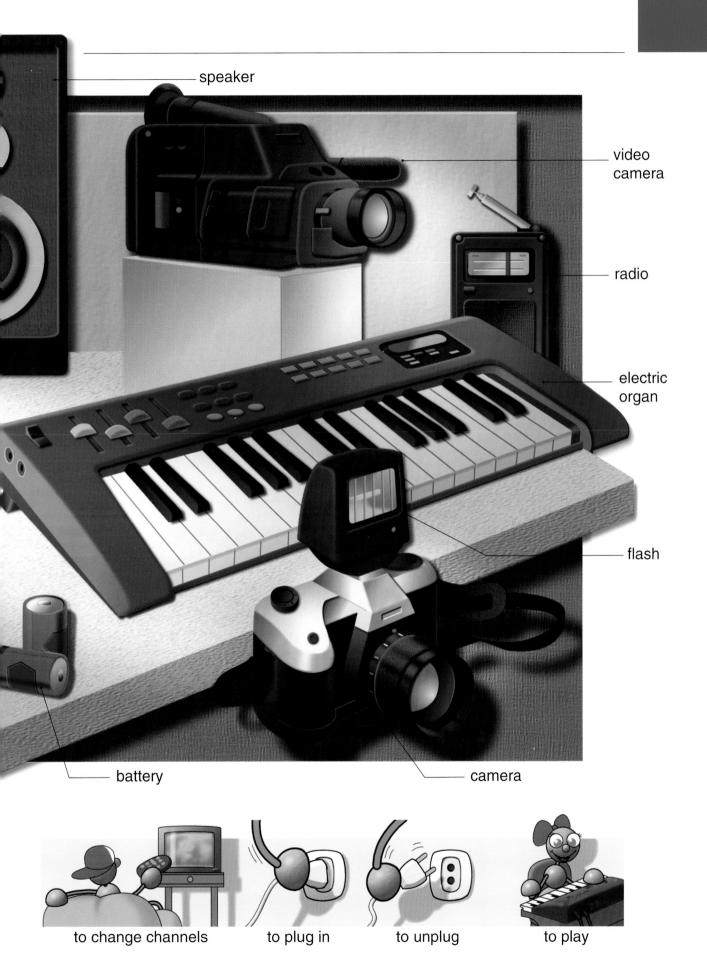

speaker

video camera

radio

electric organ

flash

battery

camera

to change channels   to plug in   to unplug   to play

At the Cinema and the Theater

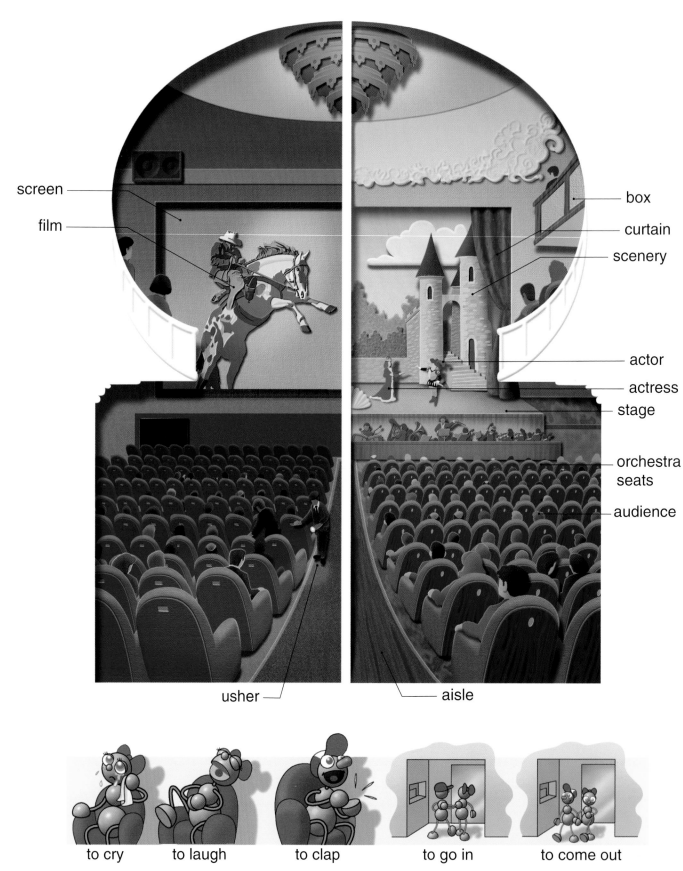

screen

film

box

curtain

scenery

actor

actress

stage

orchestra seats

audience

usher

aisle

to cry   to laugh   to clap   to go in   to come out

In the Television Studio

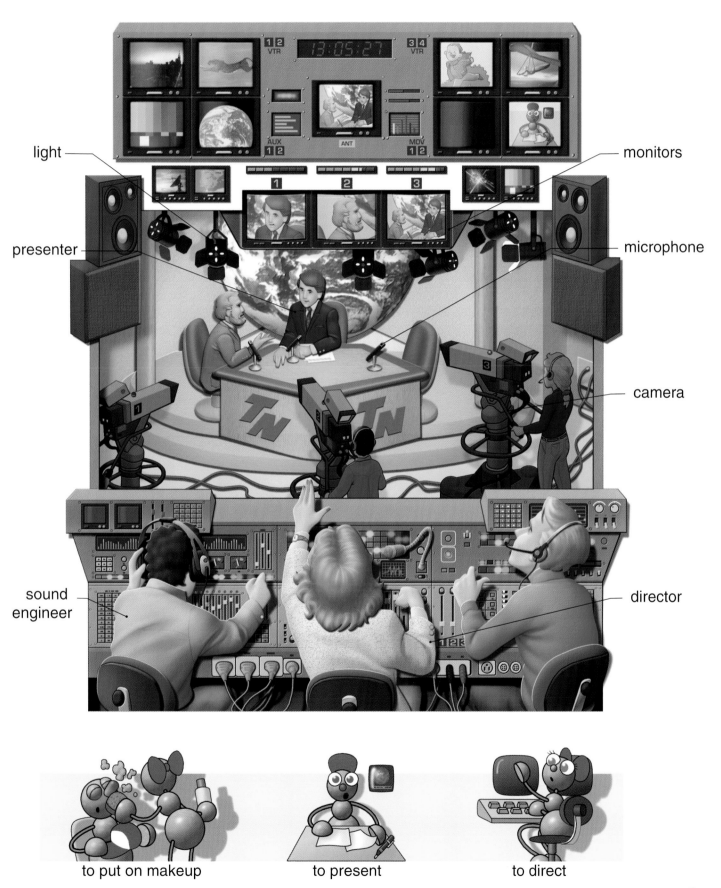

light

monitors

presenter

microphone

camera

sound engineer

director

to put on makeup

to present

to direct

Musical Instruments

electric organ

harp

piano

violin

cello

bass

xylophone

kettledrum

to sing

to dance

to tap your feet

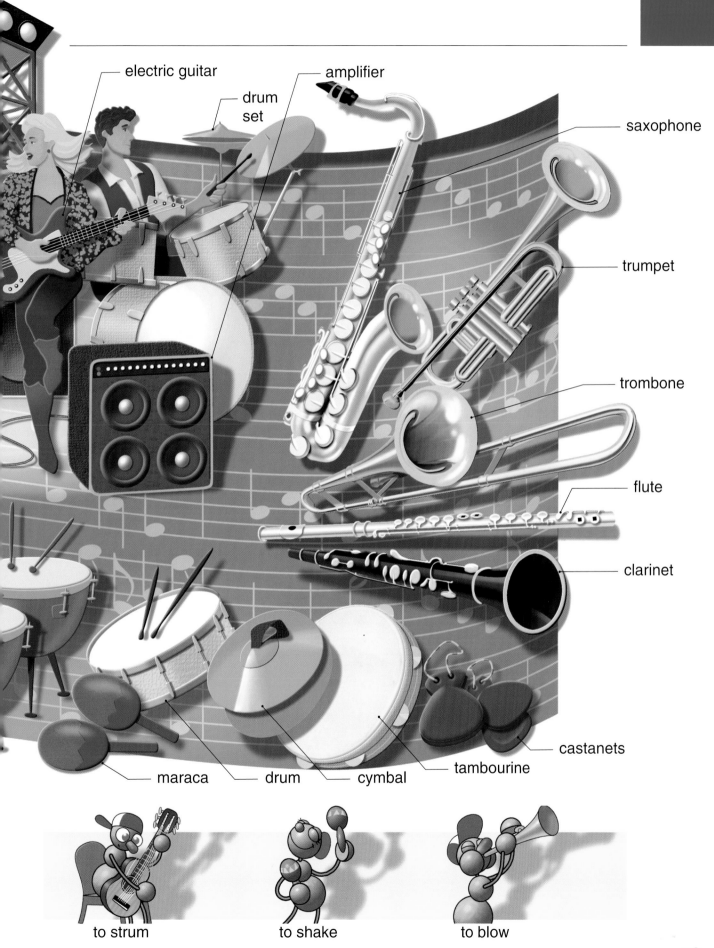

electric guitar

amplifier

drum set

saxophone

trumpet

trombone

flute

clarinet

castanets

maraca

drum

cymbal

tambourine

to strum

to shake

to blow

SPORTS
Basketball

player

ball

hoop

backboard

net

substitute

referee

umpire

bench

knee pad

basketball shoe

to bounce

to push

to score

to pass

tall

short

tired

Soccer

stadium

fans

player

post

net

goal

referee

goalkeeper

trainer

field

scoreboard

soccer ball

shirt

shin pad

cleats

linesman

bench

coach

B.F.C. 0
W.F.C. 2

to kick

to save

to throw

to blow the whistle

excited

bored

nervous

Tennis

player

racquet

wrist band

line judge

ball

net

court

to serve   to return   to hit

Swimming

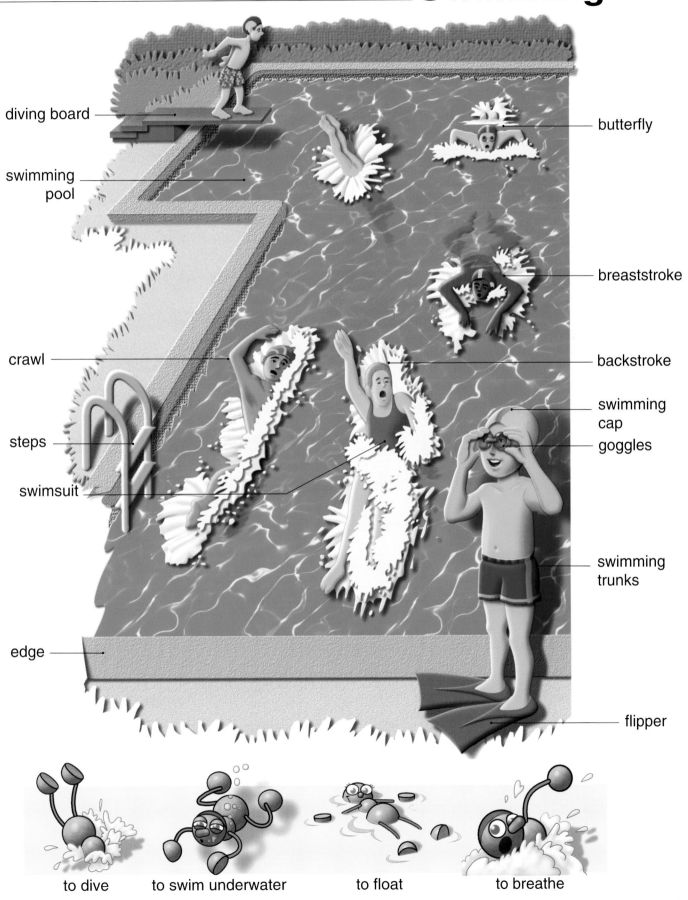

diving board

swimming pool

butterfly

breaststroke

crawl

backstroke

swimming cap

goggles

steps

swimsuit

swimming trunks

edge

flipper

to dive

to swim underwater

to float

to breathe

Skiing

ski resort

chair lift

ski slope

goggles

skier

jacket

glove

insulated pants

pole

boot

ski

to ski   to go up   to go down   to jump

Gymnastics; Track and Field

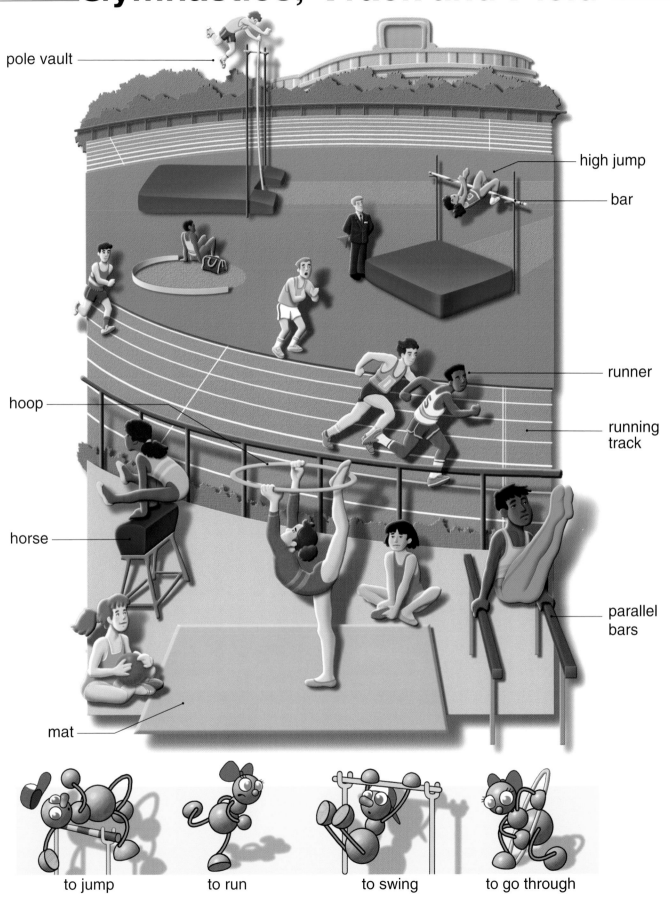

pole vault

high jump

bar

runner

hoop

running track

horse

parallel bars

mat

to jump

to run

to swing

to go through

At the Doctor's

doctor

prescription

thermometer

headache

a cold

patient

ointment

syrup

pill

capsule

to care for   to sneeze   to be sick   to examine   to cough

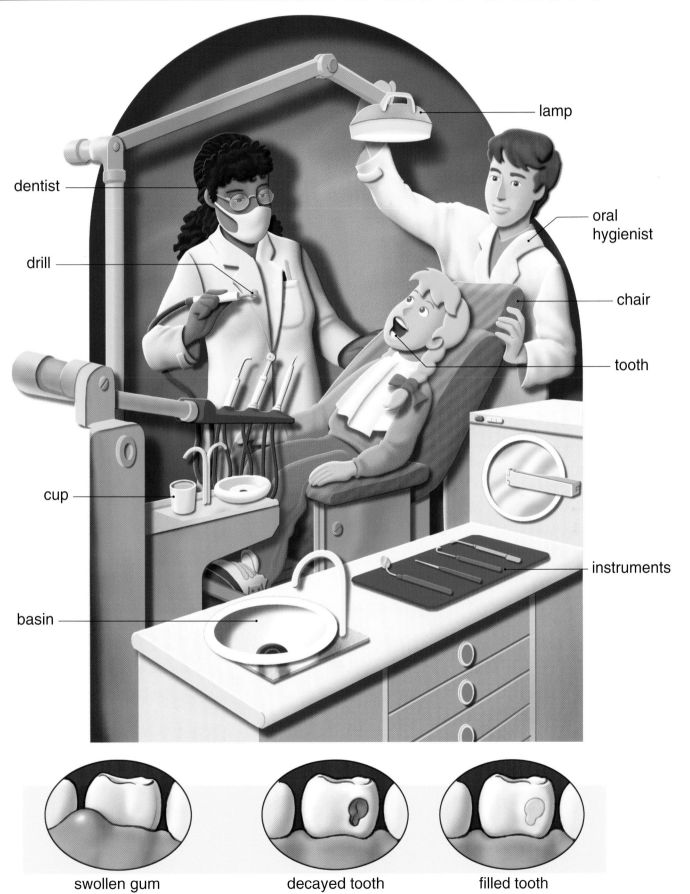

lamp

dentist

oral hygienist

drill

chair

tooth

cup

instruments

basin

swollen gum   decayed tooth   filled tooth

At the Hospital

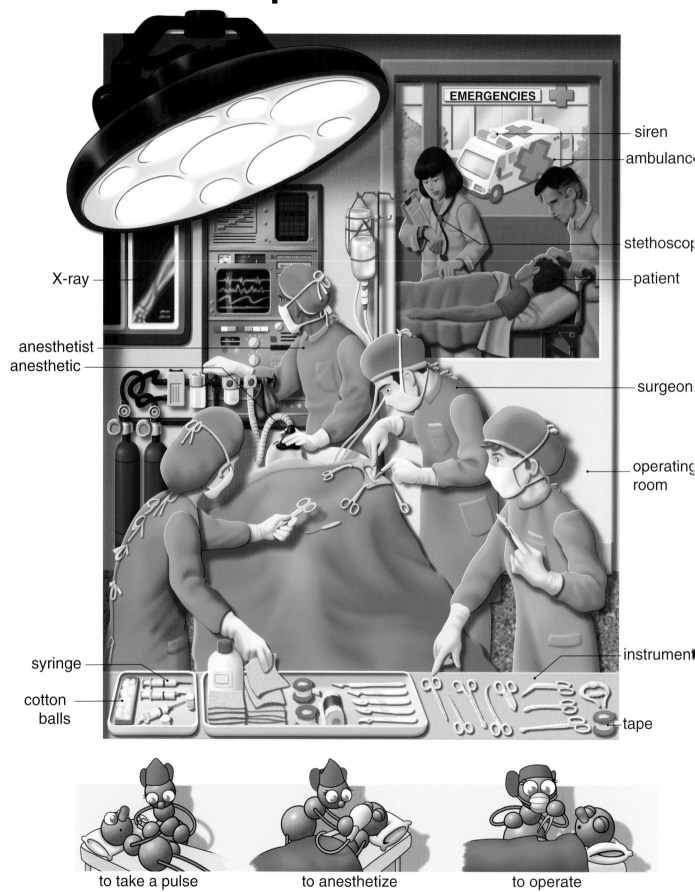

EMERGENCIES

siren

ambulanc

stethoscop

patient

X-ray

anesthetist
anesthetic

surgeon

operating
room

syringe

cotton
balls

instrument

tape

to take a pulse

to anesthetize

to operate

The Fire Department

fire engine

ladder

helmet

alarm

firefighter

hose

to rescue

to feel dizzy

to put out

At the Post Office

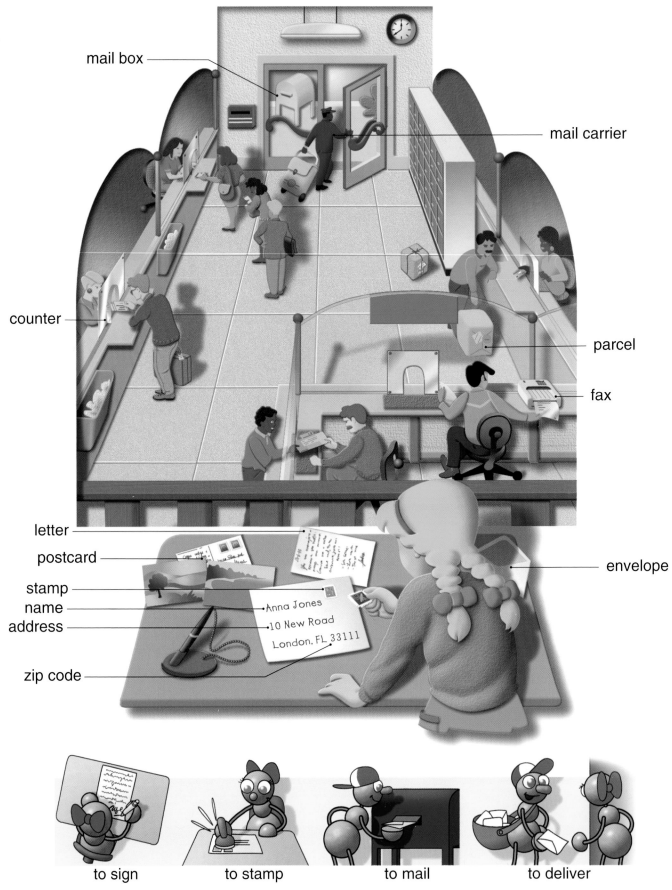

mail box

mail carrier

counter

parcel

fax

letter

postcard

envelope

stamp

name

address

Anna Jones
10 New Road
London, FL 33111

zip code

to sign

to stamp

to mail

to deliver

At the Supermarket

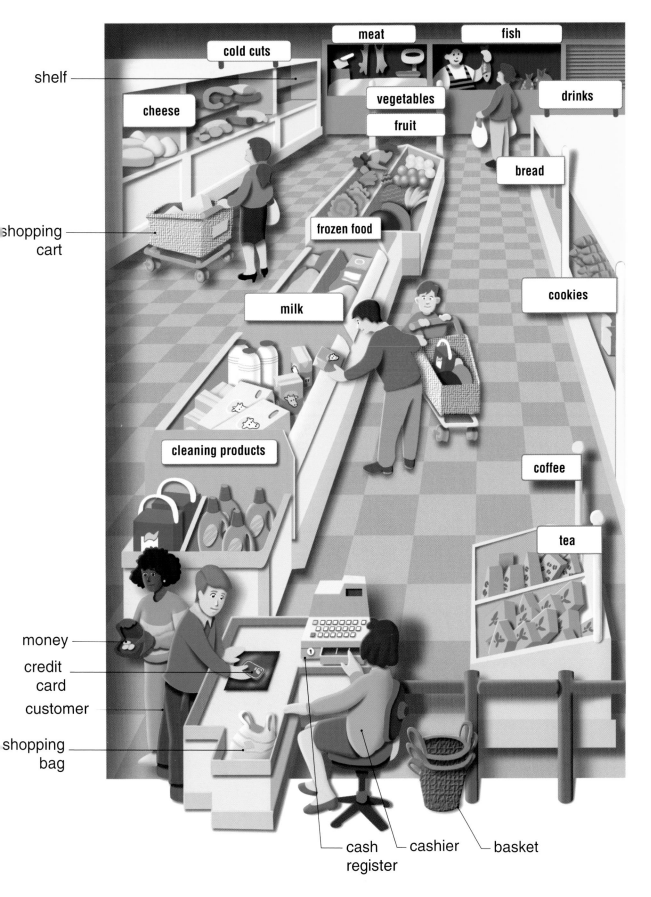

shelf

cold cuts

cheese

meat

fish

vegetables

fruit

drinks

bread

shopping cart

frozen food

cookies

milk

cleaning products

coffee

tea

money

credit card

customer

shopping bag

cash register

cashier

basket

THE UNIVERSE AND THE EARTH
The Universe

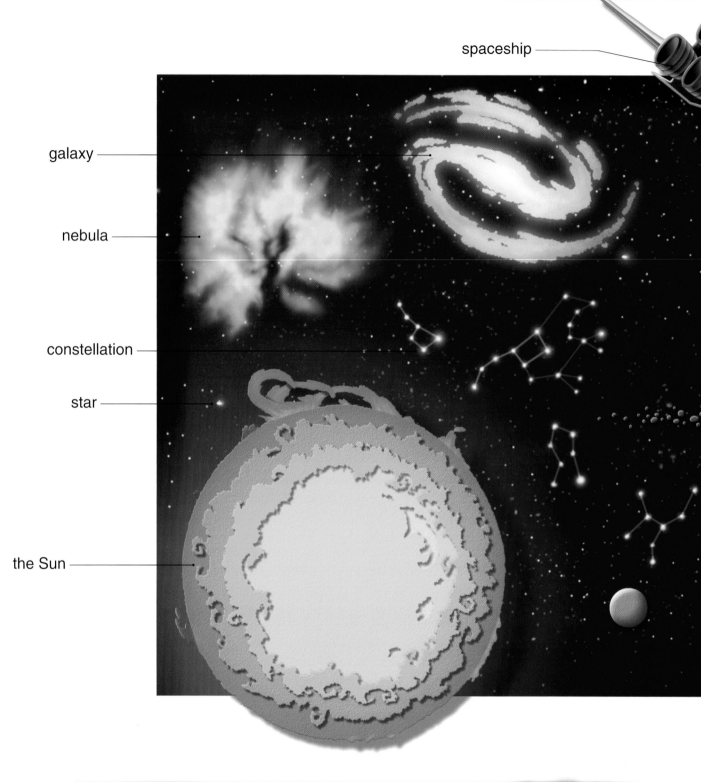

spaceship

galaxy

nebula

constellation

star

the Sun

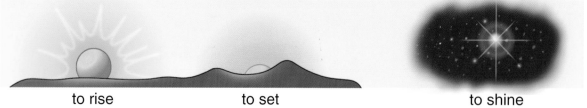

to rise

to set

to shine

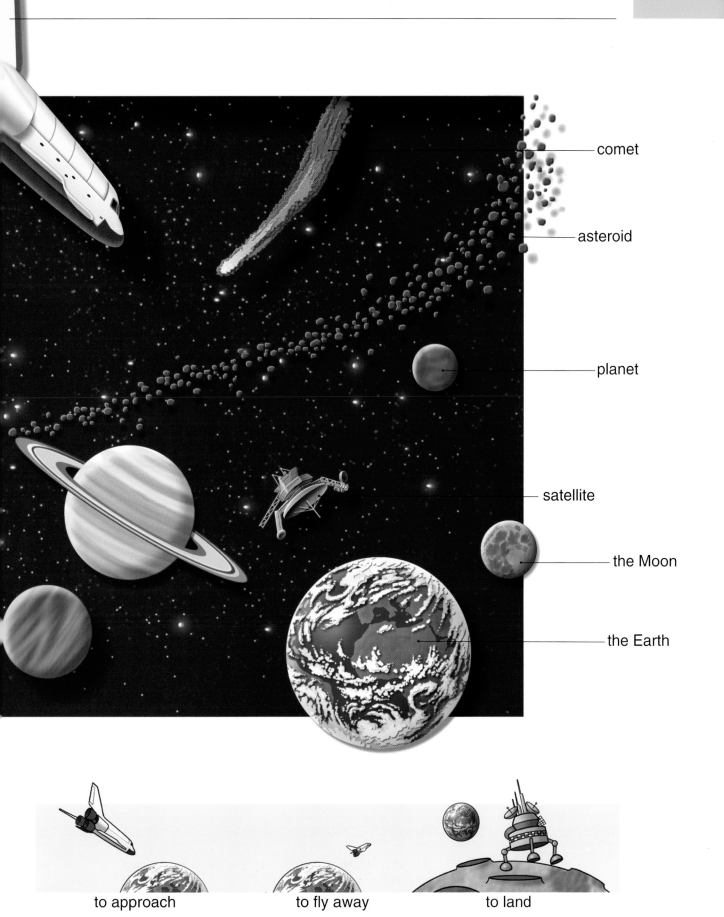

comet

asteroid

planet

satellite

the Moon

the Earth

to approach

to fly away

to land

In the Country

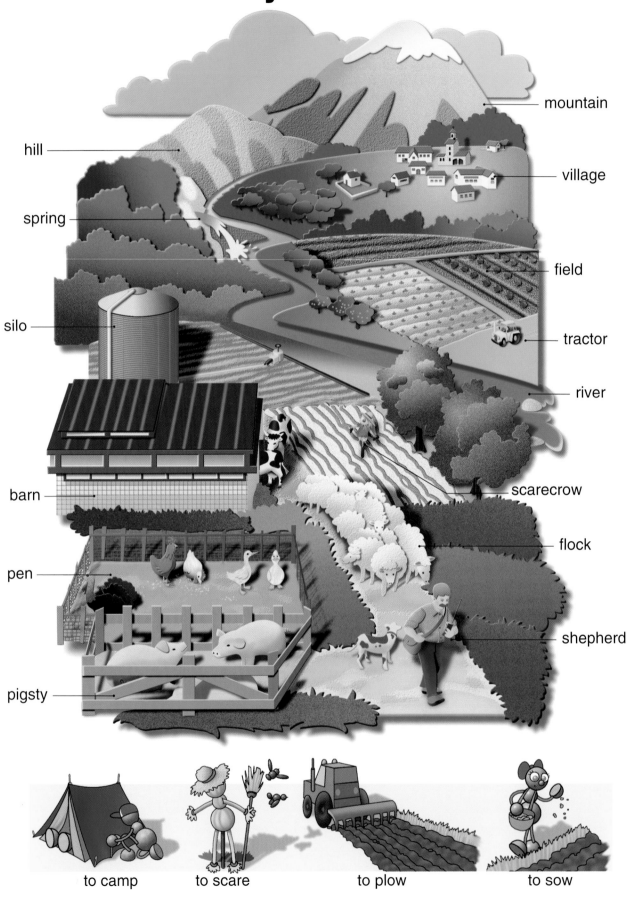

mountain

hill

village

spring

field

silo

tractor

river

barn

scarecrow

pen

flock

shepherd

pigsty

to camp

to scare

to plow

to sow

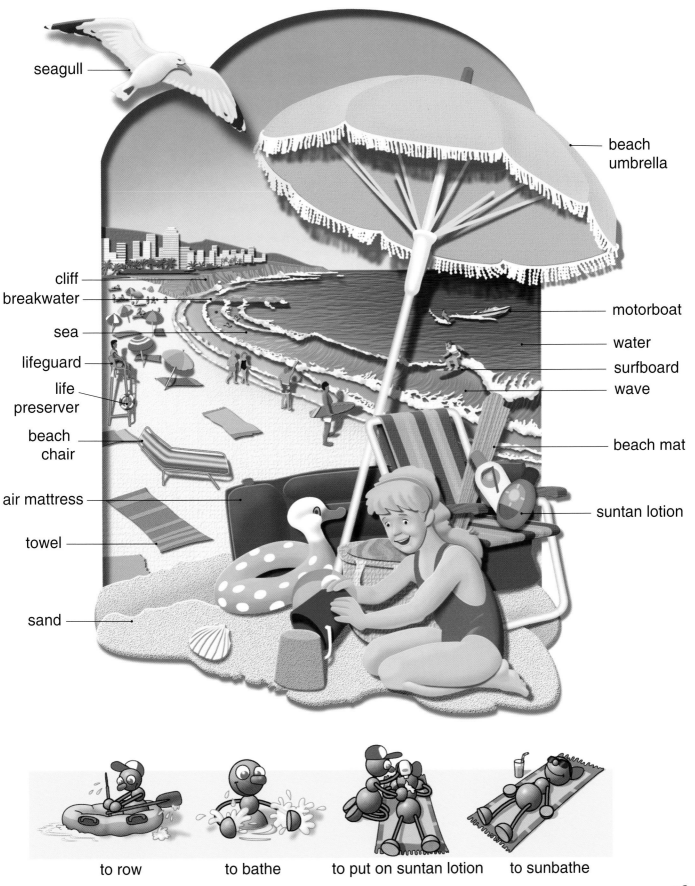

seagull

beach umbrella

cliff

breakwater

sea

lifeguard

life preserver

beach chair

air mattress

towel

sand

motorboat

water

surfboard

wave

beach mat

suntan lotion

to row

to bathe

to put on suntan lotion

to sunbathe

The Weather

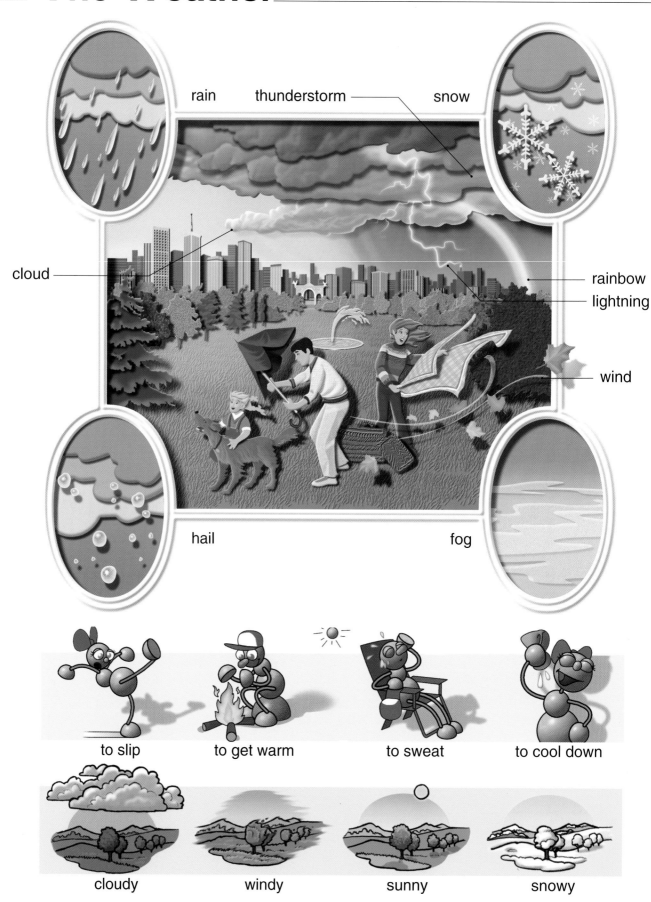

rain   thunderstorm   snow

cloud

rainbow
lightning

wind

hail   fog

to slip   to get warm   to sweat   to cool down

cloudy   windy   sunny   snowy

winter

spring

autumn

summer

to shoot

to flower

to sweep up

to pile up

autumnal

wintry

spring-like

summery

DICTIONARY

a

above: the opposite of *below*. The orange cat is above the other cats because it is high up on the back of the sofa (see page 20).

actor: a man who acts out a character in a play or film (see page 66).

actress: a woman who acts out a character in a play or film (see page 66).

to add: to put numbers together to find a total. For example, if you add one and one, the total is two (see page 26).

address: the number and name of the street and the town or city where a person lives. You write the address on the envelope when you mail a letter (see page 80).

air conditioner: a machine that controls the temperature of the air in a building (see page 15).

air mattress: a 'bed' made of rubber with air inside that people lie on when they are at the beach (see page 85).

airplane: a motor vehicle with wings that can fly. It is also called a *plane* (see page 59).

airport: the place where airplanes take off and land. It has buildings, or terminals, for passengers to wait in (see page 58).

aisle: the part of an airplane, cinema or theater where you can walk between the seats (see pages 59 and 66).

alarm: the bell that sounds to tell fire-fighters that they have to go and put out a fire (see page 79).
An **alarm clock** is a clock that makes a loud noise at a certain time to wake you up (see page 16).

almond: a small oval nut with a very hard shell (see page 44).

ambulance: a vehicle that is used to transport very sick or injured people quickly to the hospital (see page 78).

amplifier: an electrical device with speakers that makes sound louder (see page 69).

anesthetize: the medicine that makes a patient go to sleep before an operation (see page 78).

to anesthetize: to give an anesthetic to a patient (see page 78).

anesthetist: the person that gives an anesthetic to a patient (see page 78).

anchor: a piece of pointed metal at the end of a rope or chain that is thrown into the water to stop a boat or ship from moving (see page 61).

animal: a living creature. The dog, the tiger and the crocodile are all animals (see pages 28, 40 and 41).

ankle: the joint between the foot and the leg (see page 6).

antenna: a metal rod that helps a radio to work. You often see a radio antenna on a car (see page 54).

apartment: a home consisting of several rooms, usually on one floor. Flats are often found above shops, or in tall buildings (see page 48).

apple: a round fruit with a red or green skin and white inside (see page 44). An **apple tree** is the tree that apples grow on (see page 42).

to approach: to move nearer. The brown and white cat is approaching (see page 20). The spaceship is approaching the Earth (see page 83).

apricot: a small orange fruit with a furry skin and a pit in the center (see page 44).

archaeopteryx: a dinosaur with a long tail and wings like a bird (see page 29).

arm: the part of the body between the shoulder and the hand (see page 6).

armchair: a comfortable chair with 'arms' that you can sit in to relax, read or watch television (see page 15).

arrivals: the part of the information board at a station or airport that gives the time a train or plane will arrive (see page 56).

artichoke: a green vegetable in the shape of a cone. It has lots of leaves very close together (see page 45).

to ask for: in a shop, a café or a restaurant, you ask for what you want to buy or to eat (see page 48).

asparagus: a long thin green or white vegetable (see page 45).

asteroid: a rock or other material floating in space (see page 83).

to attack: dangerous or aggressive animals attack others. For example, a shark sometimes attacks people (see page 35).

audience: the people who sit in a cinema or theater to watch a movie or a play (see page 66).

aunt: a member of the family. Your mother's or father's sister is your aunt (see page 10).

autumn: the season of the year between summer and winter (see page 87).

autumnal: on an autumnal day the weather is cold, wet and windy, like in autumn (see page 87).

b

back: the reverse side of your body between the shoulders and the waist (see page 6). Many animals also have a **back** (see pages 30 and 31).
In basketball, the hoop is attached to the **backboard**. The ball can hit the backboard before it goes into the net (see page 70).
An animal that walks on four legs has two **back legs** near its tail, and two front legs near its head (see page 30).

backstroke: a style of swimming. To do the backstroke, you float on your back raising each arm in turn to move along in the water (see page 73).

baggy: the opposite of *tight*. It is easy to move if you are wearing baggy clothes (see page 13).

ball: an object that is used for playing games. Different sports use different types of balls. A tennis ball is small and round, and a football is brown and oval-shaped (see pages 70 and 72).

balloon: a colorful piece of rubber you fill with air or gas (see page 11).

ballpoint pen: an instrument for writing. It has a thin tube of ink with a small ball at the end (see page 23).

banana: a long tropical fruit with a thick yellow skin that is easy to peel (see page 44).

to bandage: to put a long piece of soft cloth around an injury (see page 52).

bank: a place where we can keep money and take it out when we need it (see page 48).

bar: a long thin piece of metal that is very difficult to bend. In the high jump, athletes try to jump over the bar (see page 75).

to bark: when a dog makes a loud noise, it barks – 'woof! woof!' (see page 30).

barn: a building on a farm for animals, such as cows or sheep (see page 84).

basin: a place to rinse the inside of our mouths at the dentist's office (see page 77).

basket: in a supermarket, you can carry the things you want to buy in a plastic or metal basket before you pay for them (see page 81).

basketball: a game between two teams. The players try to score points by putting, or shooting, a ball into a round net or basket. The players can only touch the ball with their hands (see page 70).

basketball shoe: a special shoe that basketball players wear (see page 70).

bass: a musical instrument with strings similar to a violin, but much, much bigger! (see page 68)

to bathe: to go in the ocean, lake, or swimming pool to relax or have fun in the water – not to wash! (see page 85)

bathrobe: a 'coat' you wear over your pajamas before you go to bed (see page 13).

bathroom: the room in the house where we wash and use the toilet (see page 17).

bathtub: you can wash your whole body sitting, or lying down, in a bath (see page 17).
A **bath mat** is a rug at the side of the bathtub (see page 17).

battery: the device that makes a car start and provides power for watches, radios, toys… (see pages 54 and 65).

to be sick: to throw up food from your stomach out of your mouth, when you feel ill or have eaten something bad (see page 76).

beach: a long area of sand between the land and the sea. We can sunbathe and play games on the beach (see page 85).
A **beach chair** is a 'chair' you can take to the beach to sit on in the sun. The

backs of beach chairs can be reclined (see page 85).

A **beach mat** is a long piece of material you put under a towel to lie on the beach (see page 85).

A **beach umbrella** is an 'umbrella' that people use on the beach to make shade (see page 85).

beak: the hard, pointed part of a bird's mouth (see page 33).

bear: a large, heavy animal with thick brown or black fur. Bears eat fish and meat, but also like honey. Polar bears are white (see page 41).

bed: the piece of furniture we sleep in. It usually has four legs and a mattress (see page 16).

bedroom: the room in the house where we sleep (see page 16).

bedside table: a small table or chest of drawers next to the bed where you can put books or a lamp (see page 16).

bedspread: a large piece of cloth for covering the bed (see page 16).

bedtime: the time you go to bed (see page 13).

bee: an insect which makes honey and buzzes (see page 38).

beehive: a little 'house' where bees live and make honey (see page 38).

beet: a round, dark red root vegetable (see page 45).

behind: the opposite of *in front of*. The brown and white cat is behind the cushion on the sofa (see page 21).

bell: a device that makes a noise. Some houses have a doorbell outside that you press when you want to go in (see page 14). Some bicycles also have a bell (see page 55).

below: the opposite of *above*. The brown and white cat is below the orange cat (see page 20).

belt: the long piece of leather or other material you wear around your waist. You can wear a belt to hold up pants or a skirt (see page 12).

bench: a long seat. In sports like soccer and basketball, the substitutes and the coach sit on the bench (see pages 70 and 71).

bend: a curve in the road (see page 51).

to bend: you can bend the joints in your body. For example, you bend your arm to lift a cup to your mouth (see page 7).

between: the brown and white cat is between the other two cats on the sofa (see page 21).

bicycle: a vehicle with two wheels that moves when you push the pedals with your feet (see page 55).

bidet: a small basin we sit on to wash ourselves (see page 17).

big: the opposite of *small*. A shark is a big fish (see page 35). The old bicycle in the picture has a big front wheel and a small back wheel (page 55).

birthday cake: a cake is a soft, sweet thing we eat. A cake with candles is a birthday cake (see page 11).

black: a color. The cat in the picture is black and white. Coal is black (see pages 21 and 25).

blackboard: a large rectangular board on the wall of the classroom. The

teacher writes on it with chalk
(see page 22).

blanket: a covering that we put on the bed on top of the sheets. Blankets are usually made of wool or other warm material (see page 16).

to bleat: when a sheep makes a noise, it bleats (see page 32).

blender: a small machine that mixes different ingredients together. For example, you can use a blender when you make soup (see page 18).

blind: a blind rolls up and down to cover or uncover a window (see page 16).

to blow: to make air come out of your mouth. You blow a trumpet to play it (see page 69).
The referee **blows the whistle** at certain points in a game of football (see page 71).

blue: a color. The sky is blue on a sunny day (see page 25).

board game: a game we play on a square or rectangular piece of card called a *board*. The board is usually divided into squares or other shapes. Chess and checkers are board games (see page 63).

boat: a vehicle that floats and moves through the water. A boat is smaller than a ship (see page 60).

body: the human body consists of a head, arms, legs, and other parts (see page 6). Animals also have bodies (see page 36).

to boil: to cook something in very hot water. We often boil carrots and other root vegetables (see page 45).

bones: the hard parts inside the body. The skeleton is made of bones (see page 7).

book: printed pages joined together on one side with a cover (see page 23).

bookshelves: the piece of furniture where we put books or other small objects (see page 15).

bored: the opposite of excited. When you are watching a football match with very little action, you feel bored (see page 71).

to bounce: to use your hand to make a ball go up and down. Basketball players often bounce the ball (see page 70).

bowl: a deep, round dish that we use for cereal, desserts, sauces… (see page 18).

box: a small private balcony at the side of the theater where a few members of the audience can sit (see page 66).

brachiosaurus: a very tall herbivorous dinosaur with a long neck and a small head (see page 28).

brake: a pedal or lever that makes a vehicle stop (see page 55).

to brake: to put on the brake to make a vehicle stop (see page 54).

branch: part of a tree. The branches grow out of the tree trunk. Leaves grow on the branches (see page 42).

bread: a food made from a flour dough that is baked. We use bread to make sandwiches (see page 81).
We often put pieces of bread on the table in a **bread basket** (see page 19).

breakwater: a 'wall' that goes into the sea that makes the waves less dangerous for swimmers (see page 85).

breaststroke: a style of swimming. To do the breaststroke you swim on your stomach like a frog, moving your arms and legs in a circular motion (see page 73).

to breathe: to take air into your lungs and blow it out again. You need to breathe to be able to live. When you go swimming you have to breathe correctly (see page 73).

bricklayer: a person who builds walls with bricks to make a house or other building (see page 52).

bridge: a place to cross a road or river by going over the top of it. There are bridges for pedestrians and for cars (see page 50).

brother: a member of the family. A boy is the brother of another boy or girl if they both have the same father and mother (see page 10).

brown: a color. The cat in the picture is brown. Tree trunks are brown (see pages 21 and 24).

to brush your teeth: to clean your teeth with a toothbrush and toothpaste (see page 17).

to build: to construct something. People build houses and other buildings. Bees build honeycomb (see pages 38 and 63).

bulging eyes: a frog has bulging eyes. They are very round and coming out of its face (see page 36).

bumper: the bar at the front and back of a car that protects it from damage (see page 54).

buoy: a round colored object that floats on water (see page 60).

bus: a road vehicle that carries a lot of passengers (see page 58).

butcher: a person that sells meat in a meat market (see page 52).

butterfly: a flying insect with big, beautiful wings of different colors (see page 37).
Butterfly is also a style of swimming. To do the butterfly stroke, you swim on your stomach with your head down and your arms moving in and out of the water together (see page 73).

to button: to put buttons through a slot. For example, you button a shirt when you put it on (see page 12).

to buy: when you go to a shop, you give money to buy the things you want (see page 48).

C

cabbage: a large round leafy vegetable that can be green, white or red (see page 45).

cabin: a room on a ship where passengers sleep (see page 61).
The place in a train where the engineer sits is also called a **cabin** (see page 57).
Cabin crew are the people who work on a plane and look after the passengers (see page 59).

cactus: a green plant that grows in the desert and very dry places. Be careful not to touch a cactus – cacti often have sharp thorns (see page 42).

coffee shop: a place where you go to sit and buy a drink and something to eat. A fancy coffee shop is a *cafe* (see page 48).

calculator: a small machine that we use to do mathematical calculations very quickly (see page 23).

calf: the back of the leg below the knee (see page 6).
A **calf** is also a very young cow (see page 32).

camera: the device we use to take photos (see page 65).
A **camera** is also used to film television programs (page 67).

camel: a large animal with one or two humps that lives in the desert (see page 31).

to camp: to spend the night in a tent. Some people go on camping trips (see page 84).

can-opener: a kitchen utensil for opening cans of food (see page 18).

candle: a birthday cake has candles on it. You can use a candle to give light if the electricity is not working (see page 11).

cap: a kind of hat. Baseball players wear caps. You can wear a cap to protect your eyes from the sun (see page 12).

capsule: a type of pill with plastic on the outside and medicine on the inside (see page 76).

car: a vehicle with four wheels and an engine (see page 54).
A **car racing track** is a track for racing

toy cars. Some tracks are operated by batteries (see page 63).
A **car wash** is a place we can go to wash the car (see page 54).

cardigan: a piece of clothing with long sleeves that is open at the front. Cardigans are often made from wool and have buttons (see page 12).

cards: you can play many games with cards. Cards are often rectangular and have pictures on one side. A set of cards is called a *deck* (see page 63).

to care for: to look after a person when he or she is ill (see page 76).

cargo: the things a ship transports from one place to another (see page 60).
A **cargo ship** is a large boat that carries cargo, not passengers (see page 60).
A **cargo train is** a train that carries things, not people (see page 57).

carnation: a flower that smells very sweet. It is often red, pink or white and has petals with uneven edges (see page 43).

carnivorous: an animal that just eats meat is carnivorous. Lions and tigers are carnivorous. Tyrannosaurus Rex was carnivorous (see page 29).

carrot: a long pointed orange root vegetable (see page 45).

cash register: the place in a shop or supermarket where you pay for things (see page 81).

cashier: the person who sits at the cash register and takes your cash at a store, restaurant, or supermarket (see page 81).

castanets: a musical instrument made of two round pieces of wood attached by a string. You play them by clicking the pieces of wood together in your hand (see page 69).

castle: a large stone building that people built to defend themselves hundreds of years ago. Children like to play with toy castles (see page 63).

cat: an animal with four legs, soft fur, a long tail and pointed ears. A lot of people keep cats as pets (see page 30).

to catch: to trap another creature so that it cannot escape. Fishermen catch fish. The octopus catches fish in its tentacles (see page 39).
To catch a train is to go onto a train. You go to the station to catch a train (see page 56).

caterpillar: the insect that comes out of an egg laid by a butterfly. Caterpillars turn into butterflies (see page 37).

cauliflower: a large round vegetable with a white central part and green leaves around it (see page 45).

ceiling: the part of a room above our heads (see page 16).

celery: a vegetable with a long stalk and small green leaves (see page 45).

cello: a musical instrument like a violin, but larger. You play it resting on the floor (see page 68).

cereals: grains that we eat. Corn, wheat and oats are cereals (see page 45).

chain: small pieces of metal joined together. A bicycle has a chain to make the wheels go around (see page 55).

chair: a seat with a back and usually four legs. We sit on a chair when we eat at a table (see page 15). We also sit in a special chair when the dentist examines us (see page 77).

A **chair lift** is a moving cable with chairs that carry you up a mountain if you want to ski down (see page 74).

chalk: the soft white sticks which the teacher uses to write on the blackboard (see page 22).

to change channels: when you want to watch a different program on television, you change channels. You can use a remote control to change channels (see page 65).

chard: a vegetable with green leaves and a white stalk (see page 45).

to chase: to follow something as quickly as possible to try to catch it. The snake in the picture is chasing the tortoise (see page 34).

check-in: before you travel on an airplane, you have to go to the ticket counter, where you show your ticket and check your luggage to be put on the plane (see page 58).

cheek: the part of the face next to the nose. We have two cheeks (see page 6).

cheese: a food that is made from the milk of cows, sheep or goats. There are many different types of cheeses (see page 81).

cherry: a small red fruit with a pit in the middle. It grows on trees and has a very sweet taste (see page 44).

chest: the upper part of the body that contains the lungs (see page 6).

chick: a very young hen (see page 33).

chimney: a part of the house. The chimney is on the roof and smoke comes out of it (see page 14).

chin: the part of the face under the mouth (see page 6).

chocolates: small sweets made of chocolate (see page 11).

to chop: to cut into a lot of small pieces. For example, we chop an onion to make a western omelette (see page 18).

chrysalis: before a caterpillar turns into a butterfly, it becomes a chrysalis (see page 37).

chrysanthemum: a round flower with long petals. Chrysanthemums are usually yellow or white (see page 43).

cinema: the place you can go to see movies or films (see pages 48 and 66).

circle: a round shape (see page 27).

city: a very large place where lots of people live and work. It has a lot of houses, streets, shops, public buildings… (see page 48).

clam: a creature with a round shell and a soft body that lives in the sea. We can eat clams (page 40).

to clap: to put your hands together to make a loud noise. After a play or concert finishes, the audience usually claps (see page 66).

clarinet: a musical instrument. It has a long thin black tube with silver keys. You play the clarinet by blowing into it (see page 69).

classroom: the room in a school where the teacher teaches and the pupils study (see page 22).

claw: the sharp thing at the end of some animals' toes. A hen and a tortoise have claws (see pages 33 and 34).

clay: a soft modeling material in different colors. Children play with clay to make models of many things (see page 23).

clean: the opposite of *dirty*. When your clothes are washed they are clean (see page 13).

cleaning products: things, such as detergents, that we use to clean the house (see page 81).

cleats: special shoes that soccer, baseball, and football players wear. Cleats have metal spikes on the bottom of the shoes (see page 71).

cliff: a vertical slope of rock at the edge of the sea (see page 85).

to climb: to go up something, such as a tree or a mountain (see page 62).

clipped: a hedge that has been cut is clipped (see page 46).

clippers: a garden tool for cutting hedges and other plants (see page 47).

clock: an object that tells us the time (see pages 22 and 56).

close together: two houses are close together if they are very near each other (see page 14).

closed: the opposite of *open*. A book is closed when it is on a bookshelf (see page 22).

closet: a big piece of furniture with a rail to hang your clothes on (see page 16).

clothes: shirts, pants, sweaters, and skirts are all clothes. We wear clothes to keep warm (see page 12).

cloud: a white or gray mass of water vapor that floats in the sky (see page 86).

cloudy: on a cloudy day the sky is full of clouds (see page 86).

coach: the person that shows sports players how to play, what to practice

and which exercises to do
(see page 71).

cockpit: the place in an airplane where the pilot sits (see page 59).

coffee: the dried, roasted beans of the coffee plant. The hot drink made from coffee beans is also called *coffee* (see page 81).
A **coffee-maker** is a machine that makes coffee (see page 18).
A **coffee table** is a low table where we can put a lamp, telephone, vase… (see page 15).

to coil: animals and people sometimes coil up into a round shape to go to sleep. Snakes coil up their whole bodies to stay warm and to protect themselves from their enemies (see page 34).

cold: the opposite of *hot*. Ice cream is cold (see page 9).
A **cold** is also a common illness. When you have a cold, you cough and sneeze a lot, and you usually have a sore throat (see page 76).
Cold cuts are meats that have been cooked, such as ham and salami (see page 81).

colorful: something that has a lot of colors is colorful. A butterfly's wings are colorful (see page 37).

colors: red, blue, yellow and green are all colors (see page 24).

comb: a small object with teeth that you use to comb your hair (see page 17).
A **comb** is also the red skin on top of a hen's head (see page 33).

to comb your hair: to use a comb to make your hair neat and organized (see page 17).

to come out: when a film finishes, you come out of the cinema (see page 66).

comet: a celestial body that has a glowing head and a long glowing tail. Comets move move very quickly through space (see page 83).

comfortable: the opposite of *uncomfortable*. An armchair is more comfortable than a chair (see page 15).

compass: an instrument you can use to draw a perfect circle (see page 23).

compsognathus: a small dinosaur that ran very fast on its back legs. It ate insects and small animals (see page 29).

computer: a machine with a screen, a mouse, memory and a keyboard. We use it for keeping information, for work and for playing games (see page 16).

conductor: the person on a train that looks to see that everyone has the right ticket. The conductor is also responsible for passengers' safety (see page 57).

to clean up: to put things in their proper place. You have to clean up your room if it is messy (see page 63).

cone: a shape. For example the party hat on page 11 is cone-shaped (see page 27).

constellation: a group of stars that make a shape in the sky. The Plow is a constellation (see page 82).

control tower: a building at an airport. Air traffic controllers monitor flights coming in and out of the airport from the control tower (see page 58).

cookies: cookies are sweet. They are usually round, but can be many other shapes (see pages 11 and 81).

to cool down: the opposite of *to get warm*. If you get very hot, you go to a cool place, or drink a cold drink to cool down (see page 86).

copilot: the person who sits next to the pilot and helps him or her to fly the plane (see page 59).

corkscrew: a utensil for taking the corks out of wine bottles (see page 18).

corner: where two lines or two streets join together (page 49).

cotton ball: a very soft material made of cotton. Cotton balls are used to clean cuts (see page 78).

to cough: to let out air from your lungs through your mouth making a loud noise. We cough a lot when we have a cold (see page 76).

counter: a small colored plastic disk that we use to move around a board to play a game (see page 63).
A **counter** is also the place where you go in a post office to buy stamps, send a package… (see page 80).

country: the natural landscape that is away from towns and cities. There are fields, farms, trees and animals in the country (see page 84).

court: the place where tennis is played (see page 72).

cousin: a member of the family. Your aunt and uncle's son or daughter is your cousin (see page 10).

cow: a large farm animal that gives us milk and meat (see page 32).

crab: a sea creature with a hard shell, eight legs and sharp claws (see page 40).

crane: a tall machine that is used to load cargo onto a ship (see page 60).

crash: a road accident when a vehicle crashes (see page 51).

to crash: when one vehicle hits another, they crash (see page 51).

crawl: a style of swimming. To do the crawl, you swim on your stomach and move your arms alternately in and out of the water (see page 73).

credit card: a plastic card that lets you buy things and pay for them later (see page 81).

to croak: when a frog makes a noise, it croaks (see page 36).

crocodile: a dangerous green reptile with sharp teeth and a long tail. It lives in water and on land (see page 40).

to cross: to go from one side of something to another. For example, we cross the road at a crosswalk (see page 49).

A **crosswalk** is a black and white striped path across the road where pedestrians can cross (see page 49).

to crouch: to 'sit' with your knees bent. We sometimes crouch to put on our shoes (see page 6).

to crow: when a cock (a male hen) makes a loud noise, it crows (see page 33).

to cry: babies cry when they are hungry. We cry when we are very sad, or watch a very sad movie (see pages 10 and 66).

cube: a shape. For example, dice are cube-shaped (see page 27).

cucumber: a long green vegetable that we eat sliced or chopped in salads (see page 45).

cup: we drink tea or coffee from a cup. We also use a cup at the dentist's office to rinse out our mouths (see pages 19 and 77).

cupboard: a place to put things in. It has a door, and sometimes shelves inside (see page 19).

curious: a person or animal is curious when it wants to investigate and find out about everything (see page 30).

curtain: in the theater, the curtain falls at the end of a play (see page 66).

custard apple: a tropical fruit with green skin. It is white inside with black seeds (see page 44).

customer: the person who buys things in a store (see page 81).

customs: when you arrive in a different country, you have to go through customs. Customs monitor passengers and inspect luggage and cargo (see pages 58 and 60).

to cut: to use a knife to divide something into different parts. For example, we cut our food with a knife before we eat it (see page 18). Hairdressers also **cut** hair with scissors (see page 53).
To cut out is to use scissors to cut a shape or a picture from paper (see page 22).

cymbal: a musical instrument made of a large flat metal disk. To make sound, you need to hit two symbols against each other (see page 69).

 d

dahlia: a large round flower with many petals. Dahlias are yellow, white, pink or other colors (see page 43).

daisy: a common flower with white petals and a yellow center. Small daisies often grow in grass (see page 43).

to dance: to move your body in time to music (see page 68).

dangerous: the opposite of *safe*. It is dangerous to cross the road when there is a lot of traffic (page 49).

dark: the opposite of *fair*. Dark people have black hair and brown skin (see page 6).
Dark is also the opposite of *light*. At night the sky is very dark (see page 25).

date: a sticky brown fruit with a pit in the middle (see page 44).

daytime: the time during the day, not at night (see page 12).

decayed tooth: if a tooth is bad, it is decayed. Teeth get decayed if you eat a lot of sweets (see page 77).

deck: the flat area of a ship that is in the open air (see page 61).

to decorate: to make a room look attractive with balloons and paper decorations (see page 11).

decorations: balloons and things usually made of paper that you put in your house to decorate it for a party (see page 11).

deflated: a balloon is deflated when it has no air in it. A tire is deflated when it is punctured (see page 55).

to deliver: the mail carrier delivers letters and packages to houses and offices (see page 80).

dentist: the person who examines and looks after your teeth (see page 77).

departures: the part of the information board at a train station or airport that gives the time a train or plane will leave (see page 56).

desk: a table where a pupil sits in the classroom (see page 22).

dice: the small cubes with dots on each side. One side has one dot, one side has two dots, and so on. Dice are used for playing many games (see page 63).

dictionary: a book that gives us the meanings of words. The words are listed in alphabetical order (see page 23).

to die: the opposite of *to be born.* At the end of its life, an animal or plant dies (see page 28).

different: the opposite of the *same.* The round chocolate cake and the square lemon cake are different (see page 11).

to dig: to move soil or sand from one place to another, or to make a hole in the earth with a spade (see page 47).

dining car: the part of the train that has a café or restaurant (see page 57).

dinosaurs: the very big creatures that lived on Earth millions of years ago. They are now extinct (see page 28).

diplodocus: a very tall dinosaur with a long neck. It ate leaves from the tops of trees (see page 28).

to direct: to give instructions to the people involved in a television program, movie, or play (see page 67).

director: the person who directs the making of a television program, movie or play (see page 67).

dirty: the opposite of *clean.* When our clothes are dirty they need to be washed (see page 13).

to disembark: to get off a ship (see page 61).

dishwasher: a machine that washes dirty plates, cups, spoons… (see page 19).

to dive: to jump headfirst into water (see pages 36 and 73). **To dive underwater** is to dive very deep into the water (see page 39).

to divide: in mathematics, the opposite of *to multiply.* If you divide eight by two, the answer is four (see page 26).

diving board: the rectangular board you jump or dive off at the swimming pool (see page 73).

dock: the part of a port where ships load and unload their cargo (see page 60).

to dock: a ship docks when it arrives at the port and is tied to the pier or dock (see page 60).

doctor: the person that examines you when you are ill. The doctor writes a prescription for medicines that will make you better (see page 76).

dog: an animal with four legs and a tail that a lot of people keep as a pet (see page 30).

doghouse: a small house for a dog, usually in the garden (see page 14).

doll: a toy in the form of a person, usually a baby or child (see page 63).

doll house: a toy house with small furniture in it (see page 63).

dolly: a cart with small wheels that is used in airports and train stations to carry luggage (see page 56).

dolphin: a blue-gray marine animal. Dolphins are very intelligent and friendly (see page 40).

dominoes: a game with twenty-eight pieces. Each piece has pictures, dots or blanks at each end. To play you have to put the identical pieces next to each other (see page 63).

door: the way into a house or a room (see page 14).

down blanket: a warm covering for the bed. It is usually filled with goose feathers (see page 16).

drain: a hole in the ground for water to go down (see page 49).

to drain: when we wash or cook something in water, we drain the water before we eat it (see page 45).

to draw: to make a picture on paper with a pencil (see page 24).

drill: an instrument that the dentist uses to make a hole in your tooth before filling it (see page 77).

to drink: to take in liquid. People and animals often drink water. A bee drinks nectar from a flower (see page 38).

drinks: liquids that we drink. Water, orange juice, tea and coffee are all drinks (see page 81).

to drive: to make a car move along the road (see page 54).

drone: a male bee. The drones mate with the queen bee (see page 38).

drum: a musical instrument that you play by hitting it with a stick (see page 69). A **drum set** is a group of drums of different sizes and cymbals (see page 69).

to dry yourself: when you are wet, after a bath or shower, you dry yourself with a towel (see page 17).

 e

eagle: a large carnivorous bird with a very sharp beak and claws. It has large wings and can fly very high and fast (see page 41).

ear: the part of the body at the side of the head. We have two ears and use them to hear (see pages 8 and 30).

earth: plants grow in the earth. It is also called *soil* (see page 46). The **Earth** is also the planet we live on (see page 83).

edge: the side of something. You can jump off the edge of a swimming pool into the water (see page 73).

egg: birds, insects and reptiles lay eggs. The baby creature grows inside a hard shell of the egg before it hatches (see pages 33 and 37).

eggplant: a dark purple oval-shaped vegetable that is white and has seeds inside (see page 45).

eight: a number you can also write 8 (see page 26).

eighteen: a number you can also write 18 (see page 26).

eighth: the eighth elephant in the line has the number 8 on it (see page 27).

eighty: a number you can also write 80 (see page 26).

elbow: the joint in the middle of the arm (see page 6).

electric guitar: a guitar that is powered by electricity (see page 69).

electric organ: a musical instrument like a piano, but powered by electricity (see pages 65 and 68).

electrician: a person who repairs and installs electrical things (see page 52).

electronics: machines that are powered by electricity. For example, televisions and computers are electronics (see page 64).

elephant: the biggest land animal in the world. Elephants are gray with long 'noses' called trunks (see page 41).

eleven: a number you can also write 11 (see page 26).

elm: a tall tree with a thick trunk and pointed oval leaves (see page 42).

to embark: to go onto a ship (see page 61).

emergencies: the department in a hospital for urgent cases. The part of the hospital that takes care of emergencies is called the *emergency room* (see page 78).

empty: the opposite of *full*. When you finish a glass of water, it is empty. The jar of honey is empty (see page 38).

encyclopedia: a large book or set of books with information about everything. Like a dictionary, each entry is in alphabetical order (see page 22).

engine: the motor of a car (see page 54). The **engine** is also the part of a train that contains the motor and the controls (see page 57).
An **enginer** is the person that drives a train (see page 57).
The **engine room** is the part of a ship where the engine is controlled (see page 61).

envelope: when we write a letter we put it in an envelope before mailing it (see page 80).

to erase: to use an eraser to erase a blackboard, whiteboard or chalkboard (see page 22).

eraser: a small plastic object that you use to erase pencil lines (see page 23).

to escape: if an animal is going faster than the animal chasing it, it can escape (see page 34).

to examine: to look very closely at someone or something. A doctor examines a patient very carefully to discover what is wrong (see page 76).

excited: when you are watching a very important football match and your team is winning, you feel very excited (see page 71).

exercise book: a book with blank pages that children write in at school (see page 23).

exhaust pipe: the tube at the back of a motor vehicle that fumes come out of (see page 55).

to explain: to give someone information about something. For example, the steward or stewardess on an airplane explains the safety rules to the passengers (see page 58).

eye: the part of the face we use to see. People and animals have two eyes (see pages 9, 30, 35, 37 and 39).

eyebrow: the row of hair above the eye (see page 9).

eyelashes: the row of hair along the eyelid (see page 9).

eyelid: the skin that covers the eye when it is closed (see pages 9 and 34).

to face: if two people or animals stand in front of each other, they are facing each other (see page 20).

fair: the opposite of *dark*. Fair people have light hair and skin (see page 6).

family: a mother, a father, children, grandparents, aunts, uncles and cousins all form a family (see page 10).

fans: the people who watch a soccer match or other sporting event (see page 71).

far: the opposite of *near*. For example, if you live far from school, you have to take a bus or go by car. The brown and white cat is far from you (see page 20). **Far apart** is the opposite of *close together*. Two houses are far apart when they are not near each other (see page 14).

farmer: a person who works in the country, growing fruit, vegetables and cereals, or keeping animals on a farm (see page 53).

fast: the opposite of *slow*. Racing cars go very fast (see page 54).

to fasten your seat belt: to put on your seat belt in a car or plane (see page 59).

fat: the opposite of *thin*. Some people, especially babies, are fat (see page 6).

father: a member of the family. A father is a man who has children (see page 10).

fax: a machine that can send and receive written messages. Fax machines use the telephone line. When you receive a message, it is printed on paper (see page 80).

feathers: birds have feathers covering their bodies. Each feather is a thin tube with fine hair coming from it (see page 33).

to feel dizzy: when your head feels as though it is spinning around, you feel dizzy. You can feel dizzy if you are frightened or ill (see page 79).

feelers: insects like the butterfly and the bee have feelers on their heads to feel things around them (see pages 37 and 38).

fence: a structure made of wood that surrounds a house, garden or park (see pages 14 and 46).

field: a piece of farmland containing plants or animals (see page 84). A **field is also** the rectangular piece of grass where soccer games are played (see page 71).

fierce: a fierce animal looks dangerous and can bite or scratch you (see page 30).

fifteen: a number you can also write 15 (see page 26).

fifth: the fifth elephant in the row has the number 5 on it (see page 26).

fifty: a number you can also write 50 (see page 26).

fig: a fruit with green or black skin and white inside. We often eat dried figs (see page 44).

filled tooth: a tooth that has been drilled and filled with a substance by a dentist (see page 77).

film: a story told in images and sounds that you can see at the movie theater or on television (see page 66).

to film: to use a camera to record moving images (see page 64).

fin: the part of a fish's body that it uses to control its direction in the water (see page 35).

fine: the opposite of *thick*. A paint brush is fine when it paints a very thin line (see page 25).

finger: a part of the hand. We have five fingers on each hand (see page 6).

fir: an evergreen tree that people decorate at Christmas time. Its leaves are sharp like needles (see page 42).

fire engine: the truck that firefighters use to go to a fire (see page 79).

fire department: the public service that puts out fires (see page 79).

firefighter: a person who is in the fire department and works to put out fires (see page 79).

first: the first elephant in the row has the number 1 on it (see page 26).

fish: fish are creatures that live in water. They have gills, fins and scales on their bodies. People often eat fish (see page 81).

to fish: to catch fish from the river or the sea with a net or fishing rod (see pages 35 and 53).

fisherman: a person who catches fish (see page 53).

fishing boat: a small ship used by fishermen to catch fish (see page 60).

fish seller: a person who sells fish in a fish shop. In England, fish sellers are called *fishmongers* (see page 52).

five: a number you can also write 5 (see page 26).

flamingo: a tall bird with long thin legs. Flamingoes are often pink (see page 40).

flash: if you want to use a camera indoors or in a dark place, you need to use a flash to give more light (see page 65).

flipper: a rubber or plastic 'shoe' shaped like a webbed foot. You can wear flippers to make you swim faster (see page 73).

to float: the opposite of *to sink*. To stay on the surface of the water, without touching the bottom. Boats and people can float (see pages 61 and 73).

flock: a group of sheep (see pages 32 and 84).

floor: the part of a room that is under your feet. You put rugs on the floor (see page 16).

flower: the colorful part of a plant. Flowers usually have petals and smell very sweet (see pages 43 and 46).
A **flower bed** is the part of the garden where flowers grow (see page 46).

to flower: a plant flowers when its flowers open (see page 87).

flute: a long thin musical instrument that you hold horizontally and blow into (see page 69).

to fly: to move through the air like birds. Some dinosaurs could fly. People can only fly if they go in an airplane (see pages 28 and 59).
The spaceship is **flying away** from the Earth (see page 83).

foal: a very young horse (see page 31).

fog: clouds that are very close to the ground. When there is fog, you can't see very far in front of you (see page 86).

foot: the part of the body at the end of the leg. We have two feet. We wear shoes on our feet (see page 6).

footbridge: a bridge over a road or river for people who are walking (see page 50).

forehead: the flat part of the head above the eyes (see page 6).

fork: a utensil with three or four prongs that we use for eating (see page 18).
A **fork** is also a garden tool used for moving the soil (see page 47).

forty: a number you can also write 40 (see page 26).

fountain pen: an instrument used for writing. It has a tube you fill with ink and a point, called a *nib* (see page 23).

four: a number you can also write 4 (see page 26).

fourteen: a number you can also write 14 (see page 26).

fourth: the fourth elephant in the row has the number 4 on it (see page 26).

friendly: a friendly animal likes people and is happy to see them (see page 30).

frightened: if you see a fierce dog barking at you, you feel frightened (see page 30).

frog: a small green animal that lives in water and on land. It has large bulging eyes, a sticky tongue, and webbed feet (see page 36).

frogspawn: the eggs of a frog (see page 36).

front leg: an animal that walks on four legs has two front legs, near its head, and two back legs (see page 30).

frozen food: food that we keep in the freezer, such as frozen pizza, frozen vegetables and ice cream (see page 81).

fruit: the soft part of a plant or tree we can eat. Bananas, oranges and apples are fruit (see pages 44 and 81).

to fry: to cook food in very hot oil (see page 19).

fuel: the substance that provides energy for a motor vehicle to move. Gasoline is a type of fuel (see page 58).

full: the opposite of *empty*. Before you drink a glass of water, it is full. The jar of honey is full (see page 38).

fur: the soft hair that covers the skin of animals such as cats and rabbits (see page 30).

 **g**

galaxy: a large group of stars and planets (see page 82).

to gallop: when a horse runs fast with very long steps, it gallops (see page 31).

game: a sport or activity that you play. Football and chess are games. You can also play a game with toy cars or dolls (see pages 62 and 63).

garage: a building where the car is kept (see page 14).

garbage bin: a large, heavy container for things you throw away. You can find garbage bins behind homes and businesses, like restaurants (see page 14).

garbage receptacle: a place to throw away litter, or garbage. Garbage receptacles can be in homes or on the street, and can be small or large (see page 49).

garden: the private space around a house where plants, flowers and trees grow (see pages 46 and 47).

gardener: a person who works in a garden (see page 46).

garlic: a small vegetable, similar to an onion, that is used to give flavor to other foods (see page 45).

gas station: the place where we buy gasoline for a car. Some gas stations sell groceries (see page 51).

gas tanker: a ship that carries fuel from one place to another (see page 60).

to get dressed: to put on your clothes, for example, when you get up in the morning (see page 12).

to get undressed: to take off your clothes, for example, when you go to bed (see page 12).

to get up: after you wake up in the morning, you get up and get dressed (see page 16).

to get warm: the opposite of *to cool down*. If you are cold, you can stand by a fire to get warm (see page 86).

gigantic: very, very big. Some dinosaurs were gigantic. Some animals today, like elephants and whales, are gigantic (see page 29).

gill: the part of a fish that it uses to breathe. Water passes through the gills and oxygen from the water enters the fish's blood (see page 35).

ginger: the orange color of hair or fur (see page 21).

giraffe: the tallest animal in the world. It has a very long neck, a small head and long thin legs (see page 41).

to give a present: we give presents to our friends and family at special times, such as birthdays (see page 11).

glass: a thing we drink from, usually made of a clear substance called *glass*. We drink water and orange juice from a glass (see page 18).

globe: a map of the world in the form of a sphere (see page 22).

glove: gloves are the things we put on our hands to keep them warm (see page 74).

to go away: if you walk in the opposite direction from someone, you go away from them. The brown cat is going away from you (see page 20).

to go down: you can go down some steps or a slide (see pages 14 and 62). Skiers go down the slope (see page 74).

to go in: before a movie starts, you go in the theater (see page 66).

to go through: to go from one side of something to the other. For example, a gymnast goes though a hoop (see page 75).

to go up: you go up the stairs to the floor above (see page 14). It is difficult to go up a slope wearing skis (see page 74).

goal: the net and posts at each end of a soccer field. To score a point in soccer, the players have to kick the ball into the goal. Each point they score is also called a *goal* (see page 71).

goalkeeper: the soccer player that stands in front of the goal and tries to stop the ball from going in the net (see page 71).

goggles: 'glasses' that you wear to stop water going in your eyes when you are swimming (see page 73). When you are skiing you can also wear goggles to protect your eyes (see page 74).

gorilla: the biggest member of the monkey family. It is the same size as a man and is covered in thick dark hair (see page 41).

to graft: to attach part of one plant onto another so that they grow as one plant (see page 42)

grandfather: a member of the family. Your grandfather is your mother's or your father's father (see page 10).

grandmother: a member of the family. Your grandmother is your mother's or your father's mother (see page 10).

grape: a green or purple fruit that grows in bunches. Wine is made from grapes (see page 44).

grapefruit: a large round yellow fruit with an acid taste (see page 44).

grass: the green plant that covers the surface of many gardens and parks (see page 46).

to grate: to use a grater to make something into very small, fine pieces. We can grate cheese, carrots and other foods (see page 18).

grater: a kitchen utensil with small holes that we use to grate things (see page 18).

green: a color. Leaves and grass are green (see page 24).
Green beans are long thin green vegetables (see page 45).

greengrocer: a person who sells fruit and vegetables in a shop (see page 52).

greenhouse: a 'house' made of glass where plants can grow protected from the cold and rain (see page 46).

gray: a color. The cat in the picture is gray. Elephants are gray (see pages 21 and 24).

to grow: to get bigger. All living things grow. Children grow into adults. Lambs grow into sheep, and small plants can grow into big trees (see page 42).

gymnastics: a popular sport, consisting of floor exercises, parallel bars, rings…

 **h**

hail: small round pieces of ice that sometimes fall from the clouds in a storm (see page 86).

hairdresser: a person that cuts people's hair (see page 53).

hairdryer: a small machine that blows hot air to dry your hair (see page 17).

hand: the part of the body which has five fingers and is at the end of the arm. You use your hands to pick things up (see page 6).

handlebars: the part of a bicycle or motorcycle that you hold when you are riding on it (see page 55).

hangar: the building where airplanes are kept when they are not flying (see page 58).

hanger: we put our clothes on hangers in a wardrobe (see page 16).

happy: the opposite of *sad*. You feel happy on your birthday (see page 10).

hard: the opposite of *soft*. Rocks and nuts are hard (see page 9).

hard-working: someone who works a lot is hard-working. A bee is a hard-working insect (see page 38).

harp: a large musical instrument with many strings. You sit next to the harp and play it with your hands (see page 68).

hat: a covering for the head. Berets and caps are kinds of hats (see page 12).

to hatch: when a animal comes out of an egg, it hatches (see page 28).

hazel nut: a small round nut with a hard shell (see page 44).

head: the part of the body above the neck (see pages 6, 36, 37 and 39).

headache: if your head hurts, you have a headache (see page 76).

headlight: the lights at the front of a car that light up the road at night are called *headlights* (see page 54).

headphones: the things we put on our ears to listen to music. If you are wearing headphones, other people cannot hear what you are listening to (see page 64).

health: if you are not ill, eat healthy food and exercise regularly, you are most likely in good health (see page 76).

to hear: to use your ears to receive sounds (see page 8).

hearing: one of the five senses. You need your ears for this (see page 8).

heavy: the opposite of *light*. An animal that weighs many pounds, like a hippopotamus, is heavy (see page 29).

hedge: a tall, thick line of plants that separates the yard from the street (see page 46).

helmet: a protective hat. People who ride motorcycles wear helmets (see page 55). Firefighters also wear helmets (see page 79).

hen: a farm bird that gives us eggs and meat (see page 33).

herbivorous: an animal that only eats plants, nuts and fruit is herbivorous (see page 29).

hide: the thick skin of a cow that is used to make leather for shoes and other objects (see page 32).

to hide: to keep out of sight. A small animal can hide from a bigger animal that wants to eat it (see page 39).

hide-and-seek: a game in which some children hide and others have to go and look for them (see page 62).

high jump: part of the sport of athletics. In the high jump you have to jump over a bar supported on two poles (see page 75).

highway: a very wide road with several lanes. Cars, trucks and motorcycles travel along it very fast. Other words for highway are *expressway* and *freeway* (see page 50).
A highway patrol officer is a person who wears a uniform and makes sure that people follow the rules of the road (see page 50).

hill: a feature of the landscape. If you stand on a hill you can see for a long distance. A hill is smaller than a mountain (see page 84).

hip: the part of the body at the top of the leg (see page 6).

hippopotamus: a very big herbivorous animal that lives in large rivers. It has a thick gray skin, short legs and a big head with small ears (see page 40).

to hit: to strike a ball in a sport or game. You hit the ball with a racquet in tennis, for example (see page 72).

hold: the place inside a ship where cargo is kept (see page 61).

honey: the sweet, sticky substance made by bees (see page 38).

honeycomb: the structure that bees make from wax to hold honey (see page 38).

hood: the part of a car that covers the engine. It can be opened and closed (see page 54).

hoof: the hard part of an animal's foot. Horses and sheep have hooves (see pages 31 and 32).

hoop: in basketball, the hoop is the ring that holds the net (see page 70).
In gymnastics, a **hoop** is a large ring made of plastic that the gymnasts use to do floor exercises (see page 75).

horn: the hard, sharp things that some animals have next to their ears. Bulls, cows, goats and some sheep have horns (see page 32).

horse: a large animal with a long tail, a mane and hooves. Some horses work on farms (see page 31).
Part of the equipment in gymnastics is also called a **horse** (see page 75).

hose: a long rubber tube that is attached to a tap and used to water plants in a garden (see page 47). Fire-fighters also use a hose to put out a fire (see page 79).

hospital: a large building where very ill or injured people go to get better (see page 78).

hot: the opposite of *cold*. Soup is hot (see page 9).

hotel: a place where you can stay if you are on vacation or away from home (see pages 48 and 51).

house: a building in which people live. A one-family house has one kitchen.

A house occupies the whole building (see page 14).

to hug: to put your arms around someone you like very much (see page 11).

hump: a camel has one or two humps on its back. The humps help it to live in the desert for a long time (see page 31).

hungry: when you want something to eat, you are hungry (see page 37).

hyacinth: a plant with a lot of very small flowers. Hyacinths are usually purple, blue or pink (see page 43).

hydrangea: a plant with big round blue or pink flowers (see page 43).

hyena: a wild dog. It can make a sound like laughing (see page 41).

to inspect: to look at something very closely, to see if it is legal or correct (see page 58).

instruments: the things you use to do a special job. For example, a dentist uses instruments to examine our teeth, and a surgeon uses instruments to do an operation (see pages 77 and 78).

insulated pants: the warm pants that skiers wear. Sometimes these pants have suspenders (see page 74).

iris: the colored part of the eye around the pupil (see page 9).

ironed: something ironed is not *wrinkled*. Ironed clothes are flat and neat (see page 12).

 i

in: the opposite of *out*. The brown and white cat is in the basket (see page 21). **In front of** is the opposite of *behind*. The orange cat is in front of the mirror (see pages 20 and 21).

indoor: games that you can play in the house are called *indoor games* (see page 63).

to inflate: to fill a tire with air using a special device called a *pump* (see page 55).

information board: the large notice board at a train station or airport that shows the times of arrivals and departures (see page 56).

 j

jacket: a short coat that you wear over a shirt or sweater when you go out. Jackets can be quite thin or very thick and warm (see pages 12 and 74).

jaw: the bones around the mouth are called the jaws. A shark has very strong jaws (see page 35).

jet engine: the very powerful motor that makes an airplane fly (see page 59).

jigsaw puzzle: a game with a lot of pieces you have to put together to make a picture (see page 63).

job: the occupation or work someone does for money (see page 52).

joints: the parts of the body that bend. The knee and the elbow are both joints (see page 7).

juice: a drink made from fruit (see page 11).

to jump: to go up in the air, lifting the feet off the ground at the same time. People, frogs and kangaroos can jump. In the high jump, you have to jump over a bar (see pages 6, 36, 74 and 75).

jump rope: a rope with a handle at each end. When you skip, you hold the handles and skip over the rope (see page 62).

kangaroo: an animal with a long tail and long, strong back legs. It moves by jumping. The mother carries her baby in a 'pocket' called *a pouch* (see page 41).

kettledrum: a very large drum (see page 68).

to kick: to strike something with your foot. Athletes who play soccer kick the ball (see page 71).

to kiss: to touch with the lips. We kiss people that we like (see page 11).

kitchen: a room in the house where we prepare and cook food (see page 18).

kite: a very light paper or cloth toy that flies in the wind on a long piece of string (see page 62).

kiwi: a fruit with brown fuzzy skin and a green juicy center (see page 44).

knee: the joint in the middle of the leg (see page 6).
A **knee pad** is the protective covering for the knee that sports players sometimes wear (see page 70).

knife: a sharp utensil that we use to cut things. When we eat, we often use a knife to cut our food (see page 18).

ladder: a long set of steps for climbing up or down. Firefighters use a ladder to rescue people from a burning building (see page 79).

ladle: a kind of spoon with a deep bowl that we use to serve soup (see page 19).

lamb: a very young sheep (see page 32).

lamp: a small light that you can put on a table or desk (see page 15). The dentist also has a special lamp to see into our mouths (see page 77).

to land: airplanes and spaceships land when they have finished flying and touch the ground (see pages 59 and 83).

land animal: an animal that lives on land, not in water (see page 34).

landing gear: the part of an airplane that has the wheels so planes can take off and land safely (see page 59).

lane: roads are often divided into lanes by painted lines. Highways have several lanes going in both directions (see page 50).

to laugh: you laugh when you hear a very funny story, or when you watch a comedy (see pages 10 and 66).

lawn mower: a machine that is used to cut the grass in a garden or park (see page 47).

lawyer: a person who has studied the law and defends our rights (see page 52).

leaf: the flat green part of a plant. Leaves can have many different shapes. Some trees lose all their leaves in autumn (see page 42).

to lean out: to look out of a window or balcony. It is dangerous to lean out of the windows of a train (see page 14).

leek: a long vegetable with a white root and green leaves (see page 45).

leg: the part of the body between the foot and the hips. We use our legs to walk (see pages 6, 34 and 36).

legumes: the dry, hard seeds that we cook to eat. Lima beans and lentils are legumes (see page 45).

leisure activities: things that you like to do in your free time (see page 62).

lemon: a fruit with a thick yellow skin. It is very juicy and has a very acid taste (see page 44).

lentil: a very small, round legume. Lentils can be brown, green or orange (see page 45).

leopard: a large, fierce member of the cat family. It has yellow fur with black spots (see page 41).

letter: a message you write to another person, put in an envelope and mail (see page 80).

lettuce: a green, very leafy vegetable that we eat in salads (see page 45).

library: a place that keeps lots of books. You can borrow books from a library for a certain time, and then return them (see page 48).

to lick: to move your tongue across something. Cats lick to clean themselves, and people lick ice creams (see page 30).

to lie down: people usually lie down in bed or on the beach (see pages 6 and 15).

life preserver: a ring that helps you to float in the water (see page 85).

lifeboat: a small boat that is used to rescue people at sea (see page 61).

lifeguard: a person who monitors the beach or swimming pool and rescues people in danger (see page 85).

light: the opposite of *dark*. A light color is pale, not strong (see page 25).
Light is also the opposite of *heavy*. Something that weighs very little, like a butterfly or a feather, is light (see pages 29 and 37).
A **light** is also an electrical device that is used to illuminate something. There are lights in the theater, in the television studio, and in the house (see page 67).

lighthouse: a tall building on the coast that sends light signals to ships at sea (see page 60).

lightning: the brilliant white light that appears in the sky during a thunderstorm (see page 86).

lily: a white, yellow or purple flower with open petals (see page 43).

line judge: a person that watches a game of tennis very carefully and shouts if the ball goes out (see page 72).

lima bean: a large bean with a flat oval shape (see page 45).

linesman: a person that helps the referee during a football match (see page 71).

lion: a large member of the cat family. Lions have thick yellow fur and the male has a mane around his head (see page 41).

lip: the soft outer part of the mouth. We have two lips, we use them to smile and to kiss (see pages 9 and 31).

to listen: to use your ears to hear sounds. We listen to the radio, to music, to people talking… (see page 64).

living room: a room in the house. It often has a sofa, armchairs, a television… (see page 15).

to load: to put things into a vehicle, such as luggage into a train, or boxes into a truck (see page 56).

lock: the thing we use to close a door securely. In a car we use the locks to stop the doors from opening (see page 54).

locker: a metal cupboard with a key that you can leave luggage at the bus or train station (see page 56).

long: the opposite of *short*. A jumper has long sleeves (see page 12).

to look: to use your eyes to see. Before you cross the street, you look both ways to see if cars are coming (see page 49). **To look out** is to keep looking very attentively for something. For example, when you look out for danger (see page 35).

to love: you love someone when you like them very, very much. Mothers and fathers love their children, for example (see page 10).

luggage: the bags and suitcases you carry when you travel (see page 57). A **luggage truck** is a vehicle at the airport that carries suitcases and bags to and from the plane (see page 58). A **luggage rack** is the place above the seats on a train where you can put your luggage (see page 57).

to mail: to put a letter in a mail box (see page 80).

mail box: when you want to send a letter you put it in a mail box (see pages 49 and 80).

mail carrier: a person who works for the post office delivering letters (see page 80).

mandarin: a fruit similar to an orange, but smaller and sweeter (see page 44).

mane: the long hair down the back of a horse's neck (see page 31).

map: a flat diagram that shows the geography of a city, country, or the world (see page 22).

maraca: a musical instrument. You play it by shaking it (see page 69).

marbles: the small glass balls that children play with (see page 62).

marine animal: an animal that lives in the sea (see page 34).

mat: a 'rug' used by gymnasts to do exercises on (see page 75).

meat: the flesh of an animal. Carnivorous animals only eat meat. People eat meat that is cooked (see page 81).

mechanic: a person who repairs vehicles (see page 51).

medium-sized: between *big* and *small*. The bicycle in the picture is medium-sized (see page 55).

melon: a large round fruit with a thick green or yellow skin. It is light-colored inside and contains lots of seeds. Three types of melon are cantaloupe, honeydew, and watermelon (see page 44).

to meow: when a cat makes a loud noise, it meows (see page 30).

messy: the opposite of *tidy*. A room or table is messy if it is untidy and nothing is in its place (see page 15).

microphone: the thing you speak into to record your voice or to make it louder (see page 67).

microwave oven: a small electrical oven which heats or cooks food very quickly (see page 19).

milk: the white liquid that comes from a cow. Babies drink a lot of milk (see page 81).

to milk: to take milk from a cow's udder (see page 32).

mirror: a piece of glass in which you can see a reflection (see pages 17 and 55).

to miss a train: if you arrive at the station too late, you miss the train (see page 56).

mixer: a machine used for mixing things together, such as the ingredients to make a cake (see page 18).

model: a person who wears new clothes and poses for photographers (see page 53).

modern: something that is very new is modern (see page 54).

money: the paper notes or metal coins we use to pay for things (see page 81).

monitors: the small screens in a television studio. The monitors show the director and technicians the different images being filmed by all the cameras (see page 67).

to moo: when a cow makes a noise, it moos (see page 32).

Moon: the natural satellite which goes around the Earth. We can see the Moon in the sky at night (see page 83).

mother: a member of the family. A mother is a woman who has children (see page 10).

motor: an engine that powers a vehicle or other machine (see page 55).

motorboat: a small boat with a motor (see page 85).

motorcycle: a vehicle with two wheels and a motor (see page 55).

mouth: the hole at the front of our heads that we use for eating and speaking (see page 35).

mountain: a very high place with a pointed top called a peak. The highest mountain in the world is Mount Everest (see page 84).

to multiply: in mathematics, the opposite of *to divide*. If you multiply two by three, the answer is six (see page 26).

muscles: the muscles are attached to the bones. We use our muscles to move (see page 7).

muscular: a muscular person has big, strong muscles (see page 7).

museum: a public building where you can go to see interesting collections of very old things (see page 48).

mushroom: a small round white or brown fungus with a 'cap' and a stalk (see page 45).

musical instrument: a thing you play to make music. The piano, the violin and the guitar are all musical instruments (see page 68).

mussel: a very small sea animal with a black shell and an orange body (see page 40).

 n

name: a name is what we call a person. When we send a letter, we write the person's name before we write the address (see page 80).

napkin: a square piece of paper or cloth that we use to clean our hands or mouth after we eat something (see page 19).

near: the opposite of *far*. The ginger cat is near you (see page 20).

neat: something that is arranged or orderly (see page 15).

nebula: a large cloud of light in space (see page 82).

neck: the part of the body between the head and the shoulders (see page 6). Some animals also have a neck, such as a giraffe or camel (see page 31).

to neigh: when a horse makes a noise, it neighs (see page 31).

nervous: the opposite of *calm*. You feel nervous before an exam, or when you think the other team is going to score in a soccer game (see page 71).

net: in basketball, the net hangs from the hoop (see page 70). In soccer, it forms the back of the goal (see page 71). In tennis, it goes across the middle of the court (see page 72).

new: the opposite of *old*. A new house was built very recently (see page 14).

newsstand: a place where you can buy newspapers and magazines (see page 49).

nightgown: a 'dress' that girls and women wear in bed (see page 13).

nine: a number you can also write 9 (see page 26).

nineteen: a number you can also write 19 (see page 26).

ninety: a number you can also write 90 (see page 26).

ninth: the ninth elephant in the row has the number 9 on it (see page 27).

noisy: the opposite of *quiet*. A baby is noisy when it is hungry (see page 10). A street full of cars and trucks is noisy (see page 48).

nose: the part of the face above the mouth. You smell with your nose (see page 8). The dog has a very sensitive nose (see page 30).

nostril: the two holes in the nose are called *nostrils*. You breathe and smell through your nostrils (see page 8).

notepad: sheets of paper that you can write on, joined together at the top with a piece of spiral metal (see page 23).

notice board: a board in a classroom or public place where people put information (see page 22).

number: the mathematical symbol for a quantity. For example, *1*, *2* and *3* are numbers (see page 26).

nut: nuts are the hard, dry seeds that grow on some plants. Pistachios, peanuts and walnuts are all kinds of nuts (see page 44).

 O

oak: a kind of tree. It has a wide trunk and small leaves (see page 42).

obedient: an obedient person or animal does what he or she is told (see page 32).

octopus: a marine animal with a soft body and eight 'legs' called *tentacles* (see page 39).

to oil: to put oil on something to make it work better (see page 55).

ointment: a cream for the skin (see page 76).

old: the opposite of *young*. A person who is 100 years old is old (see page 10).
Old is also the opposite of *new*. When something has existed for a very long time, it is old (see page 14).

olive tree: the tree that olives grow on (see page 42).

on: the ginger cat is on the sofa (see page 20).
On the left is the opposite of *on the right*. On the side of your left hand. The cat is on the left is close to the fish bowl (see page 21).
On the right is the opposite of *on the left*. On the side of your right hand. The brown and white cat on the right is near the fish bowl (see page 21).

one: a number you can also write 1 (see page 26).
One hundred is a number you can also write 100 (see page 26).

One million is a number you can also write 1,000,000 (see page 26).
One thousand is a number you can also write 1,000 (see page 26).

onion: a vegetable with a papery skin and white inside. Onions have a very strong taste (see page 45).

open: the opposite of *closed*. A door is open when you walk through it. A book is open when you are reading it (see page 22).

to operate: to cut open part of a person's body to make him or her better (see page 78).

operating room: the room in a hospital where operations are done (see page 78).

oral hygienist: a person who works with a dentist and who looks after patients (see page 77).

orange: a color that is a mixture of yellow and red (see page 24).
An **orange** is also a fruit with a thick orange-colored skin and a juicy middle (see page 44).

orchestra seats: the seats in a live theater that are on the ground floor and close to the orchestra (see page 66).

ostrich: the largest bird in the world. It has black and white feathers, long legs, and a long neck. It can't fly (see page 41).

out: the opposite of *in*. The orange cat is out of the basket (see page 21).

outdoor: the opposite of *indoor*. A game that we can play outside the house is an outdoor game (see page 62).
outside: the opposite of inside. The garden is outside the house (see page 14).

to overtake: to move in front of someone or something. The orange cat is overtaking the brown and white cat (see page 20). A car that is going fast can overtake a car that is going slow (see page 50).

 p

to paint: to make a picture with special colors called paints and a paint brush (see page 24).

painter: a person who paints houses (see page 53).

pajamas: the pants and shirt you wear in bed (see page 13).

palm: a tree that grows in hot places. It has very long leaves growing from its trunk. Dates and coconuts grow on palm trees (see page 42).

pansy: a colored garden flower with four petals (see page 43).

pants: clothing that covers the legs down to the ankles (see page 12).

paper clip: a small piece of metal or plastic that we use to keep papers together (see page 23).

parallel bars: two bars at different levels. Gymnasts do exercises on parallel bars (see page 75).

parasaurolophus: a dinosaur with a crest on its head, and strong teeth for eating all kinds of plants (see page 28).

parcel: an object or objects wrapped in paper, or is in a box or large envelope. To mail a parcel, you have to take it to a post office or a mail carrier can take it from a home or business. A parcel is called a *package* (see page 80).

to park: to stop a vehicle at the side of the road, or in a car park (see page 50).

parrot: a very colorful tropical bird with a large beak. Parrots can sometimes talk (see page 41).

parsley: a very leafy green plant. It is chopped and added to food to give it flavor (see page 45).

party: a party is when friends and family meet to celebrate something special, such as a birthday (see page 11).
A **party hat** is a hat made of colored paper you put on your head at parties (see page 11).

to pass: to give the ball to another player in a sport (see page 70).

passenger: a person who travels in a vehicle, not the driver (see pages 57 and 59).
A **passenger train** is a train that carries people, not cargo (see page 57).

passport: the official document you need to show when you travel to different countries (see page 58).

pastries: pies, cakes, cookies, cupcakes, cannolis and other baked goods (see page 11).

path: the place you can walk along in a garden or park (see page 46).

patient: a person who is ill or injured and who is being treated by a doctor (see pages 76 and 78).

pavement: the raised part along the side of the street that people can walk along (see page 49).

paw: paws are the feet of animals such as cats and dogs (see page 30).

pea: a very small, round, green vegetable (see page 45).

peach: a soft orange fruit with a furry skin and a pit inside (see page 44).

peanut: a small brown nut in a light shell (see page 44).

pear: a green or yellow fruit, like an apple, but with a longer shape (see page 44).

to peck: a bird pecks when it picks up small pieces of food from the ground with its beak (see page 33).

pedal: the part of a bicycle that you push with your foot. Bicycles have two pedals (see page 55).

to pedal: to push with your feet to make a bicycle move (see page 55).

pedestrian zone: a place in a town or city where cars are not permitted. Only people on foot can use it (see page 48).

to peel: to remove the skin from fruit and vegetables. For example, we peel potatoes before we cook them, and bananas before we eat them (see page 19).

pen: an outdoor space with a fence around it. Animals are sometimes kept in a pen on a farm (see pages 32 and 84).

pencil: the thing we use to draw with. Pencils are made of wood with a thin piece of graphite through the center (see page 23).
A **pencil case** is a rectangular bag often with a zipper. You use it to keep pens, pencils, erasers… (see page 23).
A **pencil sharpener** is the small thing that you use to make your pencil pointed (see page 23).

penguin: a black and white marine bird. It can't fly, but it can swim (see page 40).

petal: the flat colored part of a flower. Some flowers, like a dahlia, have a lot of petals. Some, like a pansy, only have a few petals (see page 43).

petunia: a very colorful garden flower, with an open bell shape (see page 43).

pharmacist: the person who fills prescriptions in a pharmacy (see page 53).

pharmacy: a store that sells medicine (see page 48).

photocopier: a machine that makes exact copies of papers and documents (see page 22).

photographer: a person who takes photographs (see page 53).

piano: a large musical instrument that you play by touching black and white keys (see page 68).

picture: a painting or photograph that we put on the wall to decorate a room (see page 15).

pier: another word for *dock* (see page 61).

pigsty: the part of the farm where pigs are kept (see page 84).

to pile up: to build a 'mountain' of snow, leaves, earth… (see page 87).

pill: a medicine that you take in solid form (see page 76).

pillow: when you go to sleep, it is comfortable to have a pillow under your head (see page 16).

pilot: the person who flies an airplane (see page 59).

pine: a kind of tree which has pine cones and long, thin 'leaves' called *needles* (see page 42).

A **pine nut** is the nut that grows inside a pine cone. They are sometimes used in recipes (see page 44).

pineapple: a big tropical fruit with a hard brown and yellow skin. It is very sweet and juicy inside (see page 44).

pink: a color that is a mixture of red and white. Flamingoes are often pink (see page 24).

pistachio: a very small green nut with a hard shell (see page 44).

pitcher: a container that we use to pour liquids, such as milk or orange juice (see page 19).

planet: there are nine planets that go around the Sun. The Earth, Jupiter and Saturn are all planets (see page 83).

plant: plants are living things that grow in the earth. Trees and grass are plants (see page 42).

to plant: to put a seed or young plant in the earth so that it will grow (see page 47).

plate: a round flat dish that we use to put food on. We eat pizza, fish and many other foods from a plate (see page 18).

platform: the part of a station where you stand to catch a train. Platforms have numbers and the information board tells you which platform to go to (see page 56).

to play: we play sports, like tennis or football. Children also play with toys (see page 63).

We **play** musical instruments too, like the piano and the guitar (see page 65).

player: a person who plays a sports game. There are basketball players, baseball players, hockey players, football players, soccer players, tennis players… (see pages 70, 71 and 72).

playful: a person or animal that likes to play is playful. Lambs are very playful (see page 32).

to plow: to use a special machine to break up the earth ready for sowing (see page 84).

to plug in: to connect something to the electricity supply (see page 65).

plum: a small round fruit with a red, purple or green skin. It is soft and juicy inside (see page 44).

plumber: the person who repairs and installs water pipes, sinks, washing machines… (see page 52).

poisonous: some snakes are poisonous and can inject poison when they bite. If they bite another animal, the animal can die (see page 34).

pole: the two sticks skiers use to help them balance are called *poles* (see page 74).
The **pole vault** is part of the sport of track and field. To do the pole vault, you use a long stick or pole to jump over a very high bar (see page 75).

polite: people are polite when they have good manners. A polite driver stops for you to cross the road at a crosswalk (see page 49).

poplar: a tall tree with wide heart-shaped leaves that fall in the autumn (see page 42).

port: the place on the coast or a river that ships sail to and from (see page 60).

portable stereo: a small cassette player with headphones that you can carry with you. If you have a portable stereo, you can listen to music when you are walking down the street, or on the bus (see page 64).

porter: the person who carries luggage at a station (see page 56).

porthole: the round windows on a ship are called *portholes* (see page 61).

post: the two vertical pieces of wood that hold the net in a soccer goal are called *posts* (see page 71).

post office: the place you go to buy stamps, send parcels or packages, mail letters… (see page 80).

postcard: a card with a picture on one side and space to write a short message and an address on the other side. We often write postcards on vacation (see page 80).

poster: a big printed picture that you put on the wall. There are posters of soccer teams, pop stars, animals… (see page 16).

potato: a vegetable that is brown outside and white inside. They are usually peeled before cooking. French fries are made from potatoes (see page 45).

prescription: the piece of paper with instructions to the pharmacist about the medicines you need (see page 76).

present: something special that we give to someone. Presents are usually wrapped in decorative paper (see page 11).

to present: to tell people watching television about something, such as the news (see page 67).

presenter: the person who presents a television program and who talks to the people appearing on it (see page 67).

pretty: something that is attractive to look at is pretty. For example, flowers are pretty (see page 43).

projector: a machine that shines light through a transparency so that you can see the picture on a screen (see page 22).

propeller: part of a vehicle that moves around very fast to make it go forward. Ships, planes and helicopters have propellers (see page 61).

prow: the front of a boat or ship (see page 61).

to puncture: to get a hole in a tire so that air escapes (see page 54).

pupil: the black part in the center of the eye (see page 9).
A **pupil** is also a child who goes to school (see page 22).

puppet theater: a toy theater in which you can use puppets to act out stories, called *puppet shows*. Puppets are 'dolls' that you can operate with your hands behind the theater (see page 63).

purple: a color that is a mixture of red and blue. Violets are purple (see page 25).

to push: to move something away from you (see page 15). Sometimes when a car doesn't start, you have to push it to start the engine (see page 54). You can also push a person with your hand or elbow (see page 70).

to put on: when you get dressed, you put on clothes and shoes. When you put on a cap, you place it on your head (see page 13).
To put on make-up is to 'paint' special colors or powders on a person's face (see page 67).
To put on suntan lotion is to put suntan lotion all over your body to protect it from the sun (see page 85).

to put out: you put out a fire when you make it stop burning. For example, you can put out a fire with water (see page 79).

queen bee: the largest bee in the hive. She is the only bee that can lay eggs (see page 38).

quiet: the opposite of *noisy*. When there is no noise, it is quiet. A baby is quiet when it is sleeping. A street with no traffic is quiet (see pages 10 and 48).

racquet: the thing tennis players use to hit the ball. It has a large head with strings across it (see page 72).

radar: a device that gives an instant electronic map showing the position and movement of objects, such as planes in

the sky and submarines in the sea
(see pages 58 and 61).

radiator: part of the heating system in a building. Hot water goes through pipes to the radiator and heats the room
(see page 15).

radio: a device you use to listen to music and other programs. Radios have an antenna and are powered by electricity or batteries (see page 65).
A portable **radio cassette** player is a machine we use to listen to the radio or cassettes (see page 16).

radish: a small round root vegetable. It is red outside and white inside. It is eaten uncooked and has a strong flavor
(see page 45).

rain: the water that falls down from the clouds in the sky (see page 86).

rainbow: the arch of seven colors that we see in the sky when there is rain and sun at the same time
(see pages 24 and 86).

rake: a garden tool with a long handle and a metal head at the end with lots of prongs (see page 47).

raspberry: a small red fruit that people often use to make jam (see page 44).

reading lamp: a lamp you use to give more light for studying or reading
(see page 16).

record: a round piece of flat plastic with a small hole in the middle. You put a record on a record player to listen to music (see page 16).

to record: to put sounds onto cassette
(see page 64).
A **record player** is a machine for playing records (see page 22).

rectangle: a shape similar to a square, but with two long sides and two short sides (see page 27).

rectangular: in the shape of a rectangle. A soccer field is rectangular
(see page 27).

red: a color. Tomatoes are red
(see page 25).
A **red pepper** is a large red bell-shaped vegetable. Peppers can also be green or yellow (see page 45).

referee: in sports, such as basketball, soccer and football, the referee makes sure that the players follow the rules of the game (see pages 70 and 71).

refrigerator: an electrical 'cupboard' where we keep food cold. Milk, meat, and cheese are kept in the refrigerator
(see page 18).

remote control: a small device used to change television channels from a distance (see page 64).

reporter: a person who investigates stories and writes articles for a newspaper (see page 53).

to rescue: to take someone away from a place where they are in danger
(see page 79).

to rest: to stop what you are doing for a time and relax (see page 52).

rest area: a place on the highway where you can stop to rest (see page 50).

restroom: another word for *bathroom*. We use the toilet, and wash and dry our hands in restrooms. There are restrooms in public places (see page 56).

to return: to hit a ball back to the other player in a game of tennis (see page 72).

ribs: the bones from the spine which curve around the chest (see page 7).

rice: the small white grains that are used to make a lot of different meals, such as paella and risotto (see page 45).

to ring: to make a sound with a bell. If we want to go into someone's house, we ring the doorbell (see page 15).

ripe: a fruit that is soft, sweet and ready to eat is ripe (see page 44).

river: water that runs from the land to the sea. The Amazon and the Nile are famous rivers (see page 84).

to rise: when the sun come up in the morning, it rises (see page 82).

road: the place where cars and trucks can drive (see page 49).
A **road sign** is a notice by the side of the road. Road signs give drivers information, warnings… (see page 50).

robot: a machine that looks like a person (see page 63).

roller skates: boots with wheels on the bottom. You wear roller skates to move along very quickly (see page 62).

roof: the top of a house that keeps out the rain (see page 14).

root: the part of a plant that grows under the ground (see page 42).

rose: a flower that often grows in parks and gardens. It smells very sweet, and can be many different colors (see page 43).

rotten: a fruit or vegetable that is bad, and can no longer be eaten, is rotten (see page 44).

round: in the shape of a circle. A clock face is round (see page 27).

to row: to move a small boat along by using the special 'sticks' called *oars* (see page 85).

rudder: the part at the back of a ship that controls the direction the ship goes in (see page 61).

rude: the opposite of *polite*. Rude drivers think they always have to go first (see page 49).

rug: a thick covering for the floor made from wool or similar material. Rugs can be round, square, oval or rectangular (see page 15).

ruler: a long piece of wood or plastic with centimeters, millimeters and inches marked along it. We use a ruler for measuring things or for drawing straight lines (see page 23).

to run: to use your legs to move very quickly (see pages 6 and 30). Athletes run in a race (see page 75).

runner: a person who runs in a race (see page 75).

running track: the place where running races are held (see page 75).

runway: the 'road' that airplanes use to take off and land (see page 58).

 S

sad: the opposite of *happy*. You feel sad if you don't have any friends (see page 10).

seat: the part of a bicycle where you sit (see page 55).

safe: the opposite of *dangerous*. It is safe to cross the road at a crosswalk (see page 49).

to sail: to move through water in a boat or ship (see page 60).

sailing boat: a boat with a sail that uses the wind to move (see page 60).

same: the opposite of *different*. When two things are very similar or identical, they are the same. The two pastries in the picture are the same (see page 11).

sand: the fine powder you find on a beach. Sand is usually white or yellow (see page page 85).

sardine: a small saltwater fish that people sometimes eat (see page 35).

satellite: a machine that travels around the Earth in space. Satellites are used to monitor the climate, to transmit television programs and many other things (see page 83).
A **satellite dish** is a large 'dish' that some people put on the roof of the house to receive many different television channels (see page 14).

to save: to stop a soccer ball from going into the net (see page 71).

saxophone: a musical instrument which is shaped like the letter 'J'. You blow into it to make a noise (see page 69).

scales: the small plates that cover a snake's or fish's skin (see pages 34 and 35).

to scare: to make someone frightened. Scarecrows scare away birds (see page 84).

scarecrow: a 'person' stuffed with straw and dressed in old clothes.

Farmers use scarecrows to scare birds away from their fields (see page 84).

scenery: the painted images behind the actors on stage in a theater (see page 66).

school: the place where children go to learn from the age of about four to eighteen (see page 22).
A **school bag** is a bag that children use to carry books to school (see page 23).

to score: to get a point in a sport (see page 70).

scoreboard: you can look at a scoreboard to find out how many points or goals each team has (see page 71).

to scratch: to run claws or nails over something. Cats sometimes scratch people (see page 30). Hens scratch the ground to find food (see page 33).

screen: the front part of a television set which shows programs. At movie theaters, films are projected onto a big screen (see page 66).

to scribble: to draw very quick, messy pictures (see page 24).

sea: a very big area of salt water. The Caribbean and Mediterranean are seas (see page 85).

seagull: a big sea bird with white and black or gray feathers. They catch fish to eat (see pages 40 and 85).

seal: a grey marine animal with a long body, a tail like a fish, and flippers (see page 40).

seasons: there are four seasons in the year. The seasons are spring, summer, autumn and winter (see page 87).

127

seat: the place where you sit in a vehicle or public place
(see pages 54, 55 and 57).
A **seat belt** is the strap found inside a car or other vehicle. You wear a seat belt to protect yourself in case there is an accident (see page 54).

second: the second elephant in the row has the number 2 on it (see page 26).

to see: we use our eyes to see the colors, shapes and forms of things
(see page 8).

seed: a part of the plant which is inside the fruit. New plants grow from seeds
(see page 46).

seesaw: a long board on a pivot that goes up and down. Children often play on a seesaw in the park (see page 62).

senses: we have five senses. The senses are hearing, smell, sight, taste and touch (see pages 8 and 9).

to serve: to hit the ball in a game of tennis by throwing it up in the air and then hitting it with a racquet to the other player (see page 72).

services: public institutions that help people in different ways. Examples of services include the fire department, the police department, and the post office (see page 78).

serving dish: a large plate we use to bring food to the table (see page 19).

to set: when the sun goes down at the end of the day, it sets (see page 82). When a ship begins to travel, it **sets sail** (see page 60).

seven: a number you can also write 7 (see page 26).

seventeen: a number you can also write 17 (see page 26).

seventh: the seventh elephant in the row has the number 7 on it
(see page 27).

seventy: a number you can also write 70 (see page 26).

to shake: to move something quickly up and down, or from side to side. You shake a maraca to play it (see page 69).

shaker: a small cup we use to shake dice when we play a board game
(see page 63).

shampoo: the liquid soap we use to wash our hair (see page 17).

shape: a form such as a circle, square or triangle (see page 26).

shark: a large, dangerous fish with strong jaws and sharp teeth
(see page 35).

sharp: something that cuts very well is sharp. Knives are sharp. Some animals have very sharp teeth (see page 35).

to shear: to cut the wool from a sheep (see page 32).

shed: a small wooden 'house' where gardeners keep their tools (see page 46).

sheep: a farm animal with thick wool on its body (see page 32).

sheet: a cotton covering for the bed. We sleep between sheets and under blankets (see page 16).

shelf: a flat board fixed to the wall where we put books and other objects. In a supermarket, you take the things you want to buy from the shelves
(see page 81).

shell: the hard protective 'house' on the bodies of animals such as tortoises and snails. You can also find shells at the beach (see pages 34 and 39).

shepherd: the person that looks after sheep (see page 84).

shin pad: soccer players and other athletes wear shin pads to protect the front part of their legs below the knee (see page 71).

to shine: to give light. The Sun, the stars and a light shine (see page 82).

ship: a very large boat that travels on the sea. It often has an engine (see page 61).

shirt: an item of clothing with long sleeves and buttons at the front. Shirts are often made of cotton (see page 12). A **shirt** is also something that athletes wear on the top part of their bodies to show which team they play for (see page 71).

shoe: we wear shoes on our feet to protect them when we go outside. Shoes are commonly made of leather (see page 12).

to shoot: a plant shoots when it grows new leaves (see page 87).

shop: a place where you can go to buy things. There are clothes shops, bookshops, record shops… A supermarket is a very big shop (see page 49).

shopping bag: a paper or plastic bag you use to carry the things you bought from the supermarket (see page 81).

shopping cart: a cart with small wheels that is used in stores. People use shopping carts to move many things (see page 81).

short: the opposite of *tall*. Young children are short (see pages 6 and 70). **Short** is also the opposite of *long*. A T-shirt has short sleeves (see page 12).

shorts: short pants (see page 13).

shoulder: the part of the body where the arm joins the chest (see page 6).

to shout: to say something very, very loudly (see page 10).

to show: to present something for somebody to look at. For example, we show our passports when we arrive in a different country (see page 58).

shower: the place in the bathroom where you can wash standing up. Water comes out of a lot of small holes in the shower tap (see page 17).
A **shower cap** is a plastic hat that stops your hair from getting wet in the shower (see page 17).
A **shower curtain** is the sheet of plastic that hangs by the side of the shower. It stops the floor from getting wet when you are taking a shower (see page 17).

shrimp: a very small animal that lives in the sea. It has eight legs and long feelers (see page 40).

sight: one of the five senses. You need your eyes for this (see page 9).

to sign: to write your name in your personal style (see page 80).

silo: the tall 'tower' on a farm where grain is stored (see page 84).

to sing: to produce music with your voice (see page 68).

sink: the basin in the bathroom where we wash our hands and face. Also, the round or square metal basin in the kitchen where we wash plates, bowls, knives… (see pages 17 and 18).

to sink: the opposite of *to float*. Things that are heavy or full of water can sink. Rocks sink in water because they are heavy (see page 61).

siren: the thing on top of an ambulance or police car that makes a loud noise (see page 78).

sister: a member of the family. A girl is your sister if you both have the same mother and father (see page 10).

to sit: we can sit on a chair, a sofa, a seat or on the floor (see page 15).

six: a number you can also write 6 (see page 26).

sixteen: a number you can also write 16 (see page 26).

sixth: the sixth elephant in the row has the number 6 on it (see page 27).

sixty: a number you can also write 60 (see page 26).

to skate: to move on roller skates (see page 62).

skateboard: a rectangular piece of wood with wheels. You stand on a skateboard to move along (see page 62).

skeleton: all the bones of the body (see page 7).

ski: skis are the long pointed boards that you attach to special boots when you go skiing (see page 74).
A **ski resort** is the place you stay when you go skiing. It often has hotels, cafés, shops… (see page 74).

A **ski slope** is a slope with snow prepared for skiing down (see page 74).

to ski: to go down a snow-covered slope on skis (see page 74).

skier: a person who skis (see page 74).

skiing: the sport of going down snow-covered slopes on skis (see page 74).

skin: the body is covered with skin (see pages 8 and 36).

skinny: when people are very thin and bony, they are skinny (see page 7).

skirt: girls and women wear skirts if they are not wearing pants. Skirts can be short or long (see page 12).

skull: the bones of the head (see page 7).

skyscraper: a very, very tall building in a city (see page 48).

to sleep: when you are tired, you want to go to sleep. People generally sleep about eight hours every night (see page 16).

sleeper car: a carriage in a train that has beds in it (see page 57).

slice: a triangular piece of cake, pizza, or apple (see page 11).

to slice: to cut into thin pieces. We slice cucumbers, bread and other foods (see page 45).

slide: a metal slope with steps up to it. Children like to play on a slide in the park (see page 62).

slime: the sticky liquid that a snail leaves when it moves (see page 39).

to slip: to slide and fall over on ice or other slippery surface (see page 86).

slipper: a very soft, comfortable shoe that you wear in the house (see page 13).

slippery: when something is difficult to hold because it is wet or moves a lot, it is slippery (see page 35).

to slither: snakes move by slithering along the ground (see page 34).

slow: the opposite of *fast*. The tortoise and the snail are slow animals (see page 34).

small: the opposite of *big*. The sardine is a small fish. The bicycle in the picture is small (see pages 35 and 55).

smell: one of the five senses. You need your nose to do this (see page 8).

to smell: to use your nose to find out the odor of something (see page 8).

smokestack: the 'chimney' of a ship (see page 61).

snail: a small creature with a soft body and a shell on its back. It lives in the country and in gardens (see page 39).

snake: a very long, thin creature with no legs. The cobra is a kind of snake (see page 34).

sneaker: a comfortable shoe you wear for sport or leisure. They are also called *tennis shoes* (see page 12).

to sneeze: to let air out of your nose and mouth very suddenly, making a loud noise – 'Ah-choo!'. You sneeze when you have a cold (see page 76).

snow: the soft white pieces of frozen water that fall down from the clouds (see page 86).

snowy: on a snowy day there is a lot of snow (see page 86).

soap: we use soap to wash ourselves or other things. Soap can be liquid or solid (see page 17).

soccer: a game with two teams of eleven players. Each team tries to win the game by kicking a ball into a net called a *goal* (see page 71).

soccer ball: the ball that is used to play the game of soccer (see page 71).

sock: we put socks on our feet before we put on shoes. They are often made of cotton or wool. There are knee socks, ankle socks and socks for doing different sports (see page 12).

sofa: a comfortable seat for two or more people (see page 15).

soft: the opposite of *hard*. Butter is soft. The body of an octopus is also soft (see pages 9 and 39).

son: a member of the family. A boy is the *son* of his mother and father. A girl is called a *daughter* (see page 10).

sound engineer: the person who works in a television or recording studio and controls the quality of the sound (see page 67).

soup dish: a deep plate that we eat soup from (see page 18).

to sow: to plant seeds (see page 84).

spaceship: a vehicle that travels in space. The space shuttle is a type of spaceship. It travels from and to Earth (see page 82).

spade: a garden tool with a long handle and a flat metal end. It is used for digging in the garden (see page 47).

sparrow: a small brown bird (see page 33).

speaker: the part of a record player or radio cassette that sound comes out of (see page 65).

sphere: a round shape. For example, a ball is a sphere (see page 27).

to spin: to turn your body around and around very quickly (see page 7).

spinach: a green leafy vegetable that is very good for you (see page 45).

spine: the line of bones down the back of humans and many animals (see page 7).

spiral: a twisted shape. Shells are often a spiral shape (see page 39).

sponge: we use a sponge to spread soap and water over our bodies when we bathe. Sponges are soft and take in a lot of water (see page 17).

spoon: an implement that we use for eating or serving food. We eat soup with a spoon (see page 18).

sports: competitive games such as basketball, tennis and football (see page 70).

to spray: to cover something with fine drops of liquid. We sometimes spray plants to protect them from insects (see page 42).

spring: a place where water comes naturally out of the ground (see page 84).
Spring is also one of the four seasons of the year. Spring is the season between winter and summer (see page 87).

spring-like: on a spring-like day the weather is warm and sunny, like in spring (see page 87).

square: a shape with four equal sides. A handkerchief is often square (see page 27).

squid: a marine animal with a long body and tentacles. It squirts black ink when it is frightened (see page 40).

stadium: a place where you can go to watch sports such as football. A stadium has seats for thousands of spectators (see page 71).

stage: the raised part of a theater where actors and actresses perform (see page 66).

stalk: the thin, straight part of a plant. The roots, flowers and leaves grow from the stalk. There are some stalks, like celery, that we can eat (see page 43).

stamp: when you send a letter or a postcard, you have to stick a stamp on it. A stamp is a small square or rectangular piece of paper with a picture and the price printed on it (see page 80).

to stamp: to put an ink stamp on something (see page 80).

stapler: a small device that you use to join together papers with a small piece of metal called a *staple* (see page 23).

star: we can see the stars and the Moon in the sky at night. The Sun is a star (see page 82).

starfish: a marine animal that is shaped like a star. It has five tentacles (see page 40).

station master: the person who manages a train station (see page 56).

to stay at: if you spend a night away from home, you can stay at a hotel (see page 48).

steering wheel: the wheel inside a car or truck that the driver uses to control the direction in which the truck is heading (see page 54).

stegosaurus: a large herbivorous dinosaur with hard plates along its back (see page 29).

stairs: steps on the outside of a house. Many houses have stairs that go up to the door. Stairs can also lead to the door of an airplane (see pages 14 and 59).

steps: a ladder to help people get out of a swimming pool (see page 73).

stereo system: a radio, cassette player, record player and compact disc player in one unit (see page 16).

stern: the back part of a boat or ship (see page 61).

stethoscope: an instrument that a doctor or nurse uses to listen to your chest (see page 78).

sticky: the frog has a sticky tongue. It can use its tongue to catch flying insects (see page 36).

sting: the pointed part of a bee, or other insect, that injects poison (see page 38).

to sting: a bee stings when it uses its sting to hurt another animal or human (see page 38).

to stir: to mix something into something else. When we put sugar into tea or coffee, we stir it with a spoon (see page 18).

to stop: the opposite of *to go*. Cars have to stop at a red traffic light (see page 51). Bicycles have to stop at crosswalks if people are crossing (see page 55).

straw: dry grass that animals use to make a bed or nest (see page 33).

stove: a machine that we use to cook food. Some cookers use gas, and some use electricity (see page 19).

strawberry: a small red fruit that we often eat with milk and cereal, or cream in the summer (see page 43).

street: a road with shops and other buildings in a town or city (see page 49). A **street light** is a lamp on a tall pole that lights the street at night (see page 49).

to stretch: to make something longer. We often stretch our bodies when we wake up in the morning (see page 7).

strong: the opposite of *weak*. Some animals and people are very strong. They can carry very heavy things (see page 7).

to strum: to move your fingers together across the strings of a guitar (see page 69).

studio: the large room where television programs are made (see page 67).

to study: to read, watch or listen to something to learn about it. Children study different subjects at school, such as English, math and history (see page 22).

substitute: a player that sits and waits on the side the field or court during a game. The substitute enters the game when another player is tired or injured (see page 70).

to subtract: in mathematics, the opposite of *to add*. To take one number from another. For example, if you subtract three from eight, the answer is five (see page 26).

subway: a train that goes under the ground in large cities. In some European cities, the underground is called the 'metro' (see page 48).

sucker: the octopus has suckers on its tentacles. It uses the suckers to attach itself to rocks (see page 39).

sugar bowl: a small bowl we keep sugar in (see page 19).

suitcase: a large rectangular bag that we use to carry clothes and other things in when we go on vacation (see page 56).

summer: the season of the year between spring and autumn (see page 87).

summery: on a summery day it is hot and sunny, like in summer (see page 87).

Sun: the Sun is the center of our solar system. The Earth and the other planets go around the Sun (see page 82).

to sunbathe: to lie in the sun (see page 85).

sunny: on a sunny day, the sky is blue and the sun shines (see page 86).

suntan lotion: the cream we put on our bodies in the sun to protect the skin (see page 85).

supermarket: a very big store that sells many different kinds of food (see page 81).

surfboard: a long board that people stand on to ride on the waves (see page 85).

surgeon: a doctor that performs operations (see page 78).

to swallow: to make food go from your mouth into your stomach. The shark is going to swallow the fish (see page 35).

to sweat: we sweat when we get very hot. When we sweat our skin feels wet (see page 86).

sweater: an item of clothing with long sleeves made of wool. We wear jumpers on cold days to keep us warm (see page 12).

to sweep up: to use a broom to pile up leaves or other things (see page 87).

sweet: sweets are made of sugar and can taste like strawberry, lemon, mint or other flavors. Sweets are bad for your teeth (see page 11).

Sweet corn is a type of corn. Corn is a grain that grows on large ears (see page 45).

sweet-smelling: a flower or perfume that smells very good is sweet-smelling (see page 43).

to swim: to use your arms and legs to move along in the water. Fish swim, and some animals and birds can swim (see page 28).

To swim underwater is to swim with all of your body under the surface of the water (see page 73).

swimming: a sport in which you use your arms and legs to move along in the water (see page 73).

A **swimming cap** is a rubber or plastic hat that swimmers wear to keep their hair dry or to move faster through the water (see page 73).

A **swimsuit** is the piece of clothing that people wear to go swimming (see page 73).

A **swimming pool** is a place specially built for swimming (see page 73). **Swimming trunks** are the clothing that boys and men wear to go swimming (see page 73).

swing: a seat on two ropes or chains that children sit on in the park. You swing your legs to make the seat go forwards and backwards in the air (see page 62).

to swing: to move backwards and forwards (see page 62). Gymnasts also swing from bars (see page 75).

swollen gum: the gum is the pink part at the base of a tooth. When it looks very red and gets bigger, you have a swollen gum (see page 77).

swordfish: a fish with a long pointed nose that looks like a sword (see page 40).

syringe: a tube with a needle at one end. Syringes are used to give an injection or to take blood (see page 78).

syrup: a sweet, sticky liquid. Some medicines are in the form of syrups (see page 76).

 t

table: a piece of furniture. Tables can be square, round, or rectangular. They are usually made of wood and stand on legs. We eat our meals at a table (see page 18). A **table cloth** is a large cloth we put on the table to protect it and make it look nice (see page 19).

tadpole: the young of a frog. Tadpoles are small black animals with a round body and a tail. They swim in ponds and turn into frogs (see page 36).

tail: the part of an animal that comes out of the base of its back. A kangaroo has a very long tail. A tortoise has a very short tail (see pages 30, 33, 34 and 35). An airplane also has a tail (see page 59).

to take off: the opposite of *to put on*. When you go indoors, you take off your jacket and hat (see page 13). An airplane also **takes off** when it leaves the ground and begins to fly (see page 59).

to take photos: to use a camera to make pictures (see pages 53 and 64).

to take a pulse: to put your fingers on someone's wrist to measure how fast her or his heart is beating (see page 78).

to take a shower: to use a shower to wash yourself (see page 17).

tall: the opposite of *short*. Basketball players are usually very tall (see pages 6 and 70).

tambourine: a musical instrument which you shake or tap with your fingers to make a noise. It is round with small metal disks (see page 69).

tame: the opposite of *wild*. An animal is tame when it is gentle and reacts well to people (see page 31).

tap: the place water comes from in a basin, sink or bath. We turn on the tap to get water, and turn it off when we have finished (see page 17).

to tap your feet: to hit the ground rhythmically with your feet. You usually tap your feet to music (see page 68).

tape: a long thin strip of sticky material. We use tape to stick something to something else (see page 78).

taste: one of the five senses. You need your tongue for this (see page 9).

to taste: you use your tongue to taste the flavor of things (see page 8).

taxi driver: a person who drives a taxi (see page 53).

tea: the dried leaves of the tea plant. They are used to make a hot drink which is also called *tea* (see page 81).

to teach: to explain things to pupils to help them to learn (see page 53).

teacher: a person that works in a school and teaches children subjects like mathematics, English and history (see pages 22 and 52).

teapot: we make tea in a teapot (see page 19).

teaspoon: a small spoon we use to stir sugar into tea or coffee (see page 19).

teddy bear: a toy bear that children play with and sometimes take to bed with them (see page 63).

teeth: the hard white objects in our mouths. We use our teeth to chew food. Some animals also have teeth. The singular of teeth is *tooth* (see pages 7 and 31).

telephone: a device for speaking to people who are in another place (see page 15).
A **telephone booth** is a public place where you can call somebody without hearing noises on the street (see page 49).

television: an electrical device with a screen and an antenna. We can watch movies, sports, news and other programs on television (see pages 15 and 64).
A **television studio** is the place where television programs are made (see page 67).

ten: a number you can also write 10 (see page 26).

tendons: the tendons attach the muscles to the bones (see page 7).

tennis: a sport in which two or four players compete by hitting a small ball with racquets over a net on a tennis court (see page 72).

tentacle: the eight 'legs' of an octopus are called *tentacles*. A squid also has tentacles (see page 39).

tenth: the tenth elephant in the row has the number 10 on it (see page 27).

theater: the building you go to see actors and actresses performing in a play (see pages 48 and 66).

thermometer: a very thin glass tube with mercury inside. A thermometer is used to measure your temperature when you are ill (see page 76).

thick: the opposite of *fine*. A paint brush or a book (such as an encyclopedia) can be thick (see page 25).

thigh: the top part of the leg (see page 6).

thin: the opposite of *fat*. People are thin when you can see their bones (see page 6).

third: the third elephant in the row has the number 3 on it (see page 26).

thirteen: a number you can also write 13 (see page 26).

thirty: a number you can also write 30 (see page 26).

three: a number you can also write 3 (see page 26).

three-ring binder: we put papers in a three-ring binder to organize them. It has a hard cover with three metal rings inside (see page 23).

to throw: to let something go from your hands with force. Basketball players can throw the ball (see page 71).
To throw away is to put something in a garbage receptacle when you don't want it anymore. (see page 48).

thunderstorm: a combination of heavy rain, wind, thunder (a very loud noise), and lightning (see page 86).

ticket: the small piece of paper you buy when you want to catch a train or plane. You also have to buy a ticket to go to the cinema or theater (see pages 56 and 58).
A **ticket office** is the place in a train station where you can buy a ticket (see page 56).

tidy: the opposite of *messy*. Something is tidy if everything is neat and in its place (see pages 15 and 46).

tiger: a very big member of the cat family. It has yellow and black stripes (see page 41).

tight: the opposite of *baggy*. Clothes that are tight can be uncomfortable. It is difficult to run in tight pants (see page 13).

tights: girls and women sometimes wear tights on their legs. In cold weather you can wear woolly tights to keep warm (see page 12).

tire: the black inflatable piece of rubber that surrounds a wheel (see page 54).

tired: when you finish working hard or doing a lot of exercise, you feel tired and need to sleep or relax (see page 70).

toaster: an electrical device that we put bread in to make toast (see page 19).

toe: a part of the foot. We have five toes on each foot (see page 6).

toilet: a part of the bathroom. The toilet has a seat, a cistern and a chain. We pull the chain to flush the toilet with water from the cistern (see page 17).
Toilet paper is the paper you use to clean yourself after you use the toilet (see page 17).

toll booth: the place where you pay to drive on a toll road (see page 51).

tomato: a tomato is round, red and juicy. We eat tomatoes in salads, or use them to make sauces for pizza, pasta and other foods (see page 45).

tongue: the pink muscle inside our mouths that we use to eat and taste our food (see page 9). The snake has a long sensitive tongue (see page 34). The frog has a long sticky tongue (see page 36).

tools: a gardener uses different tools to work in the garden. A spade, a rake and a trowel are tools (see page 47).

tooth: one of the hard white objects in your mouth. The plural of tooth is *teeth* (see pages 35 and 77).

toothbrush: the small brush with a long handle that we use to clean our teeth (see page 17).

toothpaste: the substance we put on a toothbrush to clean our teeth (see page 17).

tortoise: a small green animal with a hard shell on its back (see page 34).

touch: one of the five senses. You need your fingers for this (see page 8).

to touch: to put your hand or finger onto something to feel it (see page 8).

to tow: to pull a vehicle by attaching it to another moving vehicle (see page 51).

tow truck: a truck that tows vehicles away (see page 51).

towel: a soft rectangular piece of cloth that we use to dry ourselves after washing. We also use towels to lie on at the beach (see page 17 and 85).

toy: an object that children play with. Dolls and teddy bears are toys (see page 63).
A **toy car** is a small model of a car that children play with (see page 63).

track: the long metal rails that a train's wheels run along (see page 57).

track and field: a group of sports that includes running, high jump, long jump… (see page 75).

tractor: a vehicle that is used on a farm. It has very big wheels and can tow a lot of different things (see page 84).

traffic light: a light which turns red, amber (orange) or green to show drivers that they have to stop, be careful or go (see page 49).

train: a vehicle that runs on tracks. It has an engine and pulls carriages to carry passengers or things (see pages 56 and 57).

train station: the place you go to catch a train (see page 56).

trainer: a person who helps injured players by giving them a massage or other treatment (see page 71).

transportation: the different ways of going from one place to another. Trains, buses and taxis are all forms of transportation (see page 54).

tray: a flat object we use to carry food, plates, cups, and other objects, from one place to another. A tray can be round or rectangular, and made of metal, wood or plastic (see page 19).

tree: the biggest kind of plant. It has a long trunk and leaves on its branches. Apples and olives grow on trees. The pine is a kind of tree (see page 42).

triangle: a shape with three sides (see page 27).

triangular: in the shape of a triangle. Some road signs are triangular (see page 27).

triceratops: a large herbivorous dinosaur with three horns and strong teeth (see page 28).

tricycle: a small vehicle that children ride. It is similar to a bicycle, but has three wheels (see page 62).

trombone: a musical instrument made of metal that looks like a long trumpet. It has a very long section that you move with your hand to change the note (see page 69).

to trot: when a horse moves along with short, quick steps, it trots (see page 31).

trowel: a very small shovel for planting small plants (see page 47).

truck: a large road vehicle used to carry things, such as animals and machines (see page 50).

trumpet: a musical instrument made of metal that you blow into. It has long tubes and a wide end that the sound comes out of (see page 69).

trunk: the part of the back of the car where we put luggage or shopping bags (see page 54). The hard central part of a tree that the branches grow from (see page 42).

T-shirt: an item of clothing made of cotton with short sleeves. We often wear T-shirts when it's hot (see page 13).

tugboat: the small boat that guides bigger ships into port (see page 60).

tulip: a flower with six closed petals. Tulips can be red, yellow, pink and many other colors (see page 43).

tunnel: a hole through a hill or mountain that vehicles can go through (see page 50).

tureen: a deep bowl with a lid that we use to serve soup (see page 19).

to turn: to change direction. You can turn left or right in a car (see page 50). **To turn into** is to change from one form to another. For example, a tadpole turns into a frog, and a caterpillar turns into a butterfly (see page 36).

to tweet: when a bird makes a noise, it tweets (see page 33).

twelve: a number you can also write 12 (see page 26).

twenty: a number you can also write 20 (see page 26).

two: a number you can also write 2 (see page 26).

tyrannosaurus: a fierce carnivorous dinosaur with a gigantic head, very sharp teeth and small front legs (see page 29).

 **u**

udder: a cow's milk comes from its udder (see page 32).

umpire: in a game of basketball there are two umpires. One umpire monitors the time, and one umpire takes down information such as the names of the players and the number of points they score (see page 70).

to unbutton: to undo the buttons on a cardigan, shirt or coat, before taking it off (see page 12).

uncle: a member of the family. Your father's or your mother's brother is your uncle (see page 10).

uncomfortable: the opposite of *comfortable*. It can be uncomfortable to sit on a hard chair without a cushion (see page 15).

under: beneath something. The brown and white cat is under the sofa (see page 20).

underwear: clothing that people wear under their pants or skirts (see page 13).

Universe: the Universe consists of all the stars and planets that exist (see page 82).

to unload: to take things like boxes and luggage out of a vehicle (see page 56).

to unplug: to disconnect an electrical device from the electricity supply (see page 65).

unripe: when a fruit is hard and not ready to eat, it is unripe (see page 44).

untidy: the opposite of *tidy*. Something is untidy if it is messy with things in the wrong place (see page 46).

usher: the person who shows people to their seats in a cinema or theater. Ushers sometimes use flashlights if it is dark (see page 66).

utensils: all the different kinds of spoons, knives and other tools that we use in the kitchen for cooking and serving food (see page 19).

A **video cassette** is the plastic box which contains video tape (see page 64).

A **video game** is a game you play on a machine with a screen. You can hold some video games in your hand. You can also attach some video games to the television (see pages 63 and 64).

village: a very small town in the country. Villages usually consist of a few houses and a few shops (see page 84).

vintage: very old cars that people keep in collections or museums are called *vintage cars* (see page 54).

violet: a very small purple flower with a sweet smell (see page 43).

violin: a musical instrument with fine strings. You hold the violin under your chin and play it with a bow (see page 68).

 **V**

vase: a glass or ceramic pot we use to put flowers in (see page 18).

vegetable: the part of a plant, such as the root, stalk, or leaves, that we can eat. Unlike fruits, vegetables are usually not sweet (see pages 45 and 81).

veterinarian: the person who acts as a doctor for animals (see page 52).**video cassette player:** a device that records television programs and plays video cassettes (see page 64).

A **video camera** is a camera that records moving images onto video tape (see page 65).

 **W**

waist: the part of the body above the hips. You wear a belt around your waist (see page 6).

to wait: you wait at a bus stop for the bus to come. You have to wait for the lights to change before crossing the road (see page 49).

to wake up: you wake up when you stop sleeping and open your eyes (see page 16).

wall: part of a building. The walls form the outside of a house and separate the different rooms (see page 14).

to wallpaper: to stick long sheets of paper to the walls of your house (see page 14).

walnut: a brown nut with a hard, round shell and a very uneven surface (see page 44).

to wash: to clean something with water. If something is dirty, we need to wash it. We wash fruits and vegetables before we eat them. **To wash** is **also** to clean dirty dishes and cooking utensils after a meal (see pages 19 and 45).

washing machine: a machine that we use for washing dirty clothes (see page 18).

water: the sea and rivers are made of water (see page 85).

to water: to put water on a plant so that it will grow (see page 47).

watering can: a large bucket with a tube that water comes through. They are used for watering plants in the garden (see page 47).

watermelon: a very large fruit, similar to a melon, but with dark green skin, red inside, and black seeds (see page 44).

wave: waves are the 'hills' made in the sea by the wind. You need to have big waves to be able to surf (see page 85).

to wave goodbye: to move your hand to say 'goodbye' when you leave somebody (see page 59).

weak: the opposite of *strong*. People are weak when they can't lift heavy things (see page 7).

weather: the different conditions caused by the Sun, the seasons and other factors. The weather can be hot, cold, rainy, windy, sunny… (see page 86).

webbed foot: a foot with skin between the toes. Some creatures have webbed feet to help them to swim (see page 36).

to weigh: at the supermarket, customers weigh fruits and vegetables so they know how much they are buying (see page 52).

wet: something with water on it is wet. The frog's skin is wet after it jumps out of the water (see page 36).

whale: the biggest animal in the world. It lives in the sea and breathes through a hole in the top of its head (see page 40).

wheel: the round part at the bottom of a vehicle that allows it to move (see pages 54, 55 and 59).

wheelbarrow: a small cart with one wheel that a gardener uses to move soil and other things from one place to another in the garden (see page 47).

to whisk: to mix something very quickly, such as eggs for an omelette (see page 19).

whiskers: the thick hairs that grow on the faces of men and animals. A cat has long whiskers on each side of its nose (see page 30).

white: a color. The cat in the picture is black and white. Snow and polar bears are white (see pages 21 and 25).
A **white bean** is a small white legume (see page 45).

whole: a cake is whole before you cut it or eat it (see page 11).

wild: the opposite of *tame*. When an animal is not used to people, it is wild. Tigers, lions, and some horses are wild animals (see page 31).

A **wild boar** is a kind of wild pig with two tusks and thick brown hair (see page 41).

to wilt: when a flower needs water, it wilts (see page 42).

wilted: a flower that has lost its color and needs water is wilted (see page 43).

wind: air that is moving horizontally (see page 86).

window: the part of a house or vehicle that is made of glass you can look through (see pages 14, 57 and 59).

windshield: the large window at the front of a car (see page 54).
A **windshield wiper** is the thin rubber blade that moves across the windshield to clean it when it is dirty, raining or snowing (see page 54).

windy: on a windy day, there is a lot of wind (see page 86).

wing: the part of a bird's or insect's body that it uses to fly. Airplanes also have wings (see pages 33, 37, 38 and 59).

winter: the season of the year between autumn and spring (see page 87).

wintry: on a wintry day the weather is very cold and snowy, like in winter (see page 87).

wolf: a wild animal similar to a dog. It lives in groups called *packs* (see page 41).

wool: the soft hair on a sheep's back. Wool is used to make sweaters, socks and other warm clothes (see page 32).

woolly: covered in wool. A sheep is a woolly animal (see page 32).

to work: to do a job (see page 52).

worker bee: a bee that works hard to make honey and to look after the young bees (see page 38).

wrinkled: something that needs ironing is wrinkled. If you put your clothes in a pile on the floor they get creased (see page 12).

wrist: the joint between the hand and the arm (see page 6).
A **wrist band** is a piece of elastic cloth that tennis players and other sports players wear around their wrist (see page 72).

to write: to use a pen or pencil to put words on paper (see page 22).

X-ray: a special camera that can take black and white images of the inside of the body (see page 78).

xylophone: a musical instrument with metal bars that you hit with a stick to make a noise (see page 68).

yellow: a color. Lemons and bananas are yellow (see page 25).

young: the opposite of *old*. A child is a young person (see page 10).